Dear Da[illegible]
Brother, Thanks [illegible]
The Love and Mo[illegible]
On helping me
to #1 in Amazon!

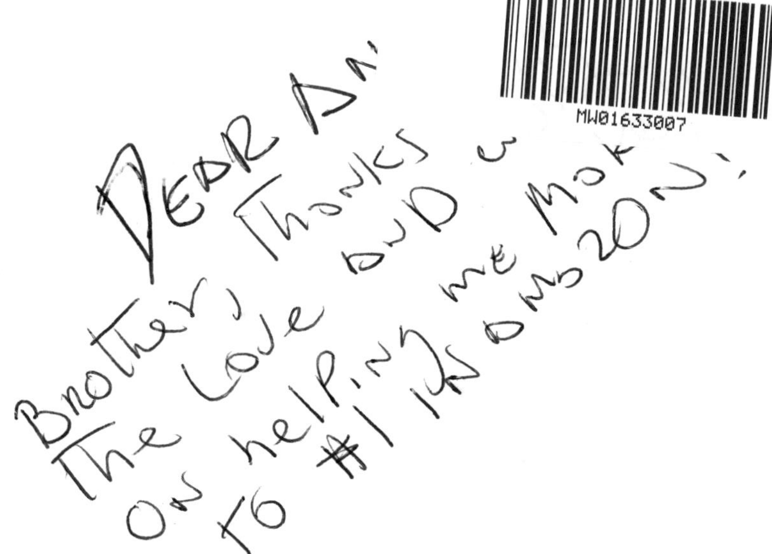

# **Breaking Out** of Corporate Jail

Since our
first meeting I had
This wonderful feeling
That our friendship
was guided by our
creator.
Blessings!!!

David
Mont[illegible]

# Breaking Out of Corporate Jail

## FIND YOUR FREEDOM
### AND TAKE CONTROL OF YOUR LIFE

DAVID MANSILLA

www.davidmansilla.com



Published by DM Publishing House.

ISBN 978-1-7772050-1-0

Book and Cover design by Natalie Mansilla

First Edition

For my wife, Shelly, my lovely kids, Ana, Jonathan, and Natalie, my youngest, a big thanks for her hard work, dedication and patience on helping me make this dream a reality.

To Felix and my beloved ISU family. Without you guys, I wouldn't be where I am today.

To all employees and entrepreneurs fighting every day to become a better version of themselves. This book is for you to help you reach your maximum potential.

To my creator for giving me the intelligence, enthusiasm and consciousness that inspired me to help others find fulfillment in their lives.

# Table of Contents

# 1

# Introduction

"For last year's words belong to last year's language
And next year's words await another voice.
And to make an end is to make a beginning."
– T.S. Eliot

If you're picking up this book because the title caught your attention, you probably picked it up at the right time in your life. Are you where you need to be? Are you going where you want to go?

To be clear, this book isn't about criticizing corporations. This book is about how you can provide massive value to the world and live life on your own terms by creating your own business.

The problem with big corporations in today's world is that they have the potential to become so giant that they begin to run like miniature governments. That's why we have anti-monopoly laws in North America. But, the root of corporations is to add value to the world. Thanks to them, people can have jobs and are able to thrive. Businesses are why the free world is moving forward. It's why we're making leaps and bounds in technological and scientific fields. However, at the same time, if you have an entrepreneurial mindset, the 9 to 5 of corporate life can be very difficult. If you have a desire in your heart and soul to do your own thing and run your own business but are trapped in a corporation, then you are in the same boat that I was in many years ago.

I was trapped in corporations for too long. I know the difficulties and stresses that come with it. However, all my corporate jobs gave me the wisdom, power, energy and experience necessary to succeed in my own business further down the line. I actually thank God for all my experiences in the corporate world. I was able to see what worked and what didn't, how office politics worked, how to manage teams, all of which are important skills to have when the time comes to fly solo. All the experiences you gain in corporate jobs are an essential part of becoming your own independent business, especially if you're aiming to have those same corporations as your target market. I've been incredibly blessed to work with a range of companies, from start-ups all the way up to big multinationals, with billions of dollars and thousands of people involved. I've really seen it all.

From my late-20s to my late-30s, I felt trapped. I thrived in each company that I worked for, but then I'd hit a ceiling and wasn't able to go any further. It was because I always wanted to do things my way since I knew there was a better, more efficient way to do them. But, sometimes, a corporation grows so big and complicated that it runs a bit slower than you want it to run. There are some deficiencies that are harder to get rid of. I'm sure you know exactly the kind of thing I'm talking about.

The aim of this book is to show you how to break out of your corporate jail job, how to start your own business, and how to add massive value to the world so that you get massive value in return. I'll tell you how I was able to thrive in life, starting out with nothing but a family I needed to feed, a big mortgage I needed to pay, and already having been made accustomed to the perks of a big corporate job; big salaries, bonuses, and vacations. My goal is to help you save ten years of your life. It's to make it possible for you to become successful faster than I was able to. It's for you to learn from all the mistakes that I've made and all the successes I've come across, so that your path can be a little less turbulent than my own.

Being an entrepreneur is one of the most rewarding things in life if you have the mentality and attitude for it. If you're an entrepreneur and it's not for you, all you'll do is struggle in life, financially, emotionally, and socially. I hope in this book I'll inspire you on your path, even if it's not necessarily starting your own business. You don't need to be your own boss to add massive value to the world. You can be utilized wherever you are right now, and your skills can be put to use no matter the level you are currently at. However, in my case, it's always been in my DNA to run on my own, and to be able to generate value, hack life, create an organization where everyone is happy and where everyone wins – not only our employees but our customers as well. This is going to be a book filled with experiences, learnings, and references to other books that I used in my life to get to where I am now.

I would like to thank you very much for your time. By reading or listening to this book, you're giving me your time, and there is no money in the world that can pay back a minute of that. But I know that time spent investing in yourself is never wasted. So, I am certain that you will get at least one thing from this material that changes your life forever.

Yours truly,

David Mansilla

davidmansilla.com

# 2

# The Beginning

*How I fell in love with computers and writing software*

"Take the first step in faith. You don't have to see the whole staircase, just take the first step."

– Martin Luther King Jr.

It was 1983 in Guatemala City. My oldest brother had been missing for over a year during a time when the country was facing major political turmoil. We were living in a civil war right in front of our eyes. There were communists and capitalists fighting against each other. The war lasted thirty years, and it was devastating for the city. At the time, I was a kid going through sixth grade when my sister started dating an airplane pilot.

My brother-in-law was a commercial airplane pilot for small passenger planes. He took me for my first flight from the city right down to the ocean. He started doing that almost every weekend, and I developed a deep passion for flying. He would go so low that I thought the wings of the plane would touch the tops of the trees. We'd go high above the ocean, and it was always so gorgeous and sunny. I couldn't believe my eyes every time we went out there together.

Because of that, I told my dad that I wanted to become a pilot. I was just a little kid about to make one of the biggest career choices of my life. My dad explained to me that becoming a private pilot was difficult, but he also told me that if I applied to military school with good enough grades and in good physical condition, the government would actually pay for my career.

So, what did I do? I started working out, swimming, and taking karate. From being an average C student, I became the best in my class. Then, I became one of the best in the school. This was all within one year thanks to the motivation of wanting to get into the academy. I wanted to get my pilots licence training so bad, and all the better if it was paid for by the government.

At the time, I didn't know this, but my dad was very happy about this decision. Back then, the war had been going on for many years already. He was starting to lose faith that we would ever find my brother, which we sadly never did. He was always of the opinion that it was better to be trained and sent to war than to get drafted without any training only to die in the mountains. So, for him, it was safer for me to become part of the military because he didn't want to lose another son.

The school I wanted to get into was one of the most prestigious schools in the country – it was where all the officials graduated from. I really applied myself and just barely passed my exams. It was extremely difficult, but it was one of the most pivotal decisions in my life. It gave me discipline and the ability to have a laser-beam focus on what I wanted.

When I was in the second year of military school, however, I got some bad news. The military announced that they wouldn't be training any more pilots since they had more pilots than they had airplanes. My only choice was to become an airplane mechanic, which I didn't like at all, or to become an official and go to the navy or the army. Both would have been difficult career paths, but neither of them was my calling. I was only there to become a pilot.

While I was going through this transition, we had to pass a typing exam. Before computers, there were these things called typewriters, and we had to take a course on them in order to graduate from military school. I took the course and I found it devastating that if I made a small mistake in a word, I had to start from scratch! Sometimes the document was several pages long, and if I made a single mistake, I had to start all over. I knew that there had to be a better way.

At the time, my uncle was a senior manager in the IT department at one of the biggest banks in the country. In passing conversation, I told him about the problem I had in my typing course. I complained about how inefficient and frustrating it was to have a small mistake render all my work useless. He thought for a second before saying, "Let me show you a solution I have at my office ". Out of curiosity, I went to visit him at work, and he showed me a computer terminal. I remember it was black and green. He showed me a text editor and said "Check it out: I can make a mistake and delete it. If I want to print, I press this button and it prints. If I want copies, I press it 10 times. Everything at the bank is managed by computers ".

I was beyond amazed. I was so frustrated with type writing that this sudden revelation blew me out of the water. He inspired me so much, and I didn't realize it right away, but this discovery would completely change the direction of my life. My uncle showed me how the bank used it to keep track of loans, checks, balances, and he told me that this process was called business automation. I couldn't believe it.

I told my dad that I fell in love with computers. And you know what my dad did? My dad went about three months later to buy an apple II computer. This computer was so old (back then, it was revolutionary) that it didn't have a graphical user interface! It was a text-based apple computer. Can you imagine that? He bought the computer, locked it in his home office, and he would always make sure that I'd see where he hid the key. He told me never to use the computer, *ever.* I was a teenager back then, so what do you think I did? Every time he'd leave the house, I'd find the key and play with the computer.

I eventually became so proficient with the computer that by the end of my second year of military school, I told my dad that I wanted to change courses and take computer science. The initial disappointment of not becoming a pilot faded pretty quickly. I now had a new passion to pursue. I asked my dad to help me get into the best school we could afford. He was really happy about that decision. He and my uncle both started researching what my best option would be. My uncle had experience hiring junior developers, and he already knew where to go. The problem was that this school, thanks to it being the best, was also one of the most expensive schools in town. I was very lucky to have my dad.

He was always passionate about cars. He had about seven cars when his passion was at its prime. He loved to fix them, upgrade them, and use them. When he understood how much it would cost for me to go to this school, he gave up two of his cars to get the down payment for my tuition. And I got in.

The school was *really* hard, but it gave me so much. My passion completely changed from airplanes to computers, and I got totally immersed in it. This school gave me what I needed to become a professional developer, and it was also the setting that God gave me to meet my wife and my best friends, who I'm still best friends with thirty years later. We still talk every day, and we get to see each other every once in a while. And I'm still married to the same beautiful lady. I met her the second year of computer science school.

You know, it's funny because the only reason I fell in love with computers was because I didn't want to do the type writing. If you boil it down, it was always laziness that inspired my motivation for computers. But I'd soon learn that it wasn't all about taking it easy. As soon as I went to school, it was super hard. We started learning C Language, Basic, and Pascal. It was incredibly difficult because while it was the best computer school, it was also one of the hardest schools for math and physics.

I started to find ways to automate everything in my life using computers. I became the assistant of the computer lab manager. Back then, no one had personal computers. I was one of the few in the country that had one. Everything had to be done in a computer lab, with a mainframe and a terminal. I became good friends with the manager of the computer lab at the school, so I had easy access to the lab. Because I was in love with automation, I would stay two- or three-hours past school to learn how to do the operations, how to copy files, and how to manage things.

Don't get the wrong idea. I was obsessed with computers, but I definitely wasn't a computer genius – *yet.* I was actually always the worst in computer science class. All my friends were better than me. Today, out of five guys, two of us stayed in computer science and we're currently working together. My buddy is my VP of operations. Everyone else followed different career choices. Even though they were better than me, it simply wasn't their passion. It wasn't in their DNA. They applied their intelligence to other skills in life. Me, I was the worst, but I was so focused on learning it that I'm still running my software development business to this day. And that's how I got started.

I had graduated from computer science school in Guatemala. In the same month I got my diploma, my dad became the CEO of a manufacturing plant. They were doing injected plastic molds for different uses like shampoos, sprays, etc. They were making all kinds of bottles for the industry. He had 300 employees, and they were writing checks by hand. He said to me, "Ok, now you know some programming. I've got a computer at the office and I need you to write me a payroll system ". Of course, I took on the challenge. It was a chance for me to apply what I learned in the real world. I hired one of the smartest kids in school, and together over three months, I had made my first commercial product. It was a very rudimentary payroll system, but it ran well, it had a database, and it was calculating contributions and deductions for employees while printing checks automatically. What took the payroll department a week to accomplish, we cut down to one day. That was one of the first amazing experiences I had with computer science and applying it to business.

Once we had all of this in production, my older brother was already in Canada. He went to study at business school because he wanted to become his own boss, too. He got this scholarship to go to Laurier University, and he opened his own business on his last year of school. His business skyrocketed. He started importing goods and crafts from exotic countries, with the target market of women ages 14 to 60. It took off. It was the first store like this in the city. With business, there always comes a need for automation.

He was having a lot of problems trying to do the invoices and inventories. He was trying to do it all by hand. By now, it was 1991. He went back to Guatemala on vacation. My dad took him back to the factory, and he showed him the system that I built for him. My brother asked me if I wanted to come to Canada to write an invoicing system for him, because they were going crazy going to bed at midnight or 1am just counting the invoices and fixing all the mistakes they made. Of course, I agreed.

A lot of what shaped who I am and where I am today happened between Guatemala and Canada. I saw a humungous opportunity to move to Canada, but my brother was a struggling student and I was just starting my own career as a software engineer. I also had my beautiful wife and a one-year old baby. I was blessed enough to have had a car that was worth something and one of my best friends helped me sell my car to his dad. I got the tickets figured out, and I thought that was enough, but it really wasn't. I had a student loan from university that I had just finished, and I forgot that I needed some money for provisions until I got to my brother's house in Canada. The thing is I only had enough money to see my sister in the United States – she lived in New York City back then. My brother was supposed to pick me up at the border.

Me and my dad threw a going away party, just a small reception to say goodbye. My uncle, my dad, and my aunt were all there. My wife's family was there, too. At the end of the night, my aunt – I don't know how or why –came and gave me fifty US dollars. She said, "Gatito," – that's what they nicknamed me, it's Spanish for little cat – "take this money and use it in case of an emergency. God knows you might need it." I took the money and put it in my wallet. That was the only cash I had on hand. All the money went to buying the tickets, so that was all the money I had. I flew to New York City, and in 1991, it was not the same as it is now. It was a very scary place back then. I stayed with my sister for a couple of days and she showed me around. I told my wife, "If Canada is like this, we're getting a plane back the next day." Even though I was coming from a country that was suffering a civil war, some parts of the city looked scarier than Guatemala did. After a couple of days, my sister put me on a bus to Buffalo to meet my brother.

Remember those fifty bucks? As soon as I left my sister's house, we were on a ten-hour bus ride, and my baby daughter started to cry. She needed food, and we didn't have any for her. The bus took a quick stop at a gas station and I was able to use that money to provide food for my daughter, wife and myself. We bought some diapers too, and that held us over while we got to Buffalo. Once we were there, we found out that my brother couldn't pick me up (remember, he was struggling, too). He figured out with his friend that we could go to a convent to wait for him. We didn't have any money for a hotel or anything like that.

We knocked on the door of this convent, and sure enough, these kind nuns took us in. We were just two crazy kids trying to get to Canada, and we stayed there with them for a while. That was the first time that I experienced true compassion in my life from people that didn't even know me. These women of faith took us in and gave us their love. I started washing dishes and my wife was doing other chores in exchange. We stayed there for two weeks and we made beautiful friends. It was an incredible experience. Up to today, I'm still so grateful for them, because they showed us mercy and compassion when we needed it the most.

After those two weeks, my brother was finally able to fix his car and come pick us up. He came, we hugged each other, and we were finally in Canada. This was one day before my wife's birthday, November 17, 1991. That's how we made it. By the way, I still have ten bucks from those fifty my aunt gave me. Huge lesson learned: if you really want to do something, and you want it with all your heart, God will always show you the way and give you the path to achieve it. Obstacles are a way to get through life and become a better person. Problems make you better.

I wrote his first Point of Sales system from scratch, and then I realized that my English wasn't good enough. I didn't have the cultural skills to survive in Canada, let alone to thrive.

Once we were settled into Canada, I realized that the education from back home wasn't regarded in the same way although the qualifications were the same. We made a conscious decision with my wife that I needed to go back to school. Thankfully, my brother was living in a university town, which to this day still has one of the best computer science and business schools in the country. I reviewed all the courses and I decided to go with the best course for practical computer science, as I already had my bachelor's degree from back home. I wanted to become more of a commercial developer.

I was accepted into all the programs, but I went with the fastest route because I needed to maintain my family. So, we made an agreement with my wife. I told her, I was going to go back to school and then she would get the chance to go back to school as well after I got a stable job or launched my own business. I started computer science school in early 1992, and it completely changed my life for the better. I had a grandfather who was an accounting auditor, and my dad had run several businesses by himself, and they both advised me that I should take as many accounting courses as I could while keeping my computer science as a major. I was destined to write business software.

I thrived in all my subjects since I already had the education from Guatemala, but in the accounting world, it wasn't as easy. I also took a few graphic design courses. Of course, the most difficult one for me was business communications, which was basically English for business. I remember I had to take business communications 1 and 2 if I wanted to graduate. It was so hard for me that I decided to go into full immersion. I took both of them in summer school. I didn't have the luxury to stop school in the summer like most other students did. I needed to get out as fast as possible, so I could move forward with my life and continue to support my family.

Thankfully, I was still working part-time with my brother, so I was able to go to school and have a steady income. That's how I survived during those years. When I first started my business communications course, it was crazy. Our professor had a PhD in English and she was an amazing communicator, but this also meant that she was very strict with us. Needless to say, if you look at my transcript, most of them are A and A+, especially in the computer science areas, but I had a couple of C's that were from my business communications courses. Having said that, it was one of the most important skills that I needed to acquire in order to start a career for myself in this beautiful new country.

All this time, I continued working with my brother and kept enhancing the Point of Sales system. My brother's company started to grow, so multiple locations were opening across southern Ontario, and I took my brother on as my major project for my final in school. My job ended up helping me finish my education. Back then, I was able to get dialup modems – if you're old enough, you'll know what that is. It's how we communicated before the internet. It's dialed up using a BBS server. I created a centralized database system where all the stores would dump all the data overnight using an automated dialup script and it would produce central reporting for him. I finished that project in 1994, just a few months before I graduated in 1995. I received the highest grade in the program because my project was already contributing a solution to a real-world problem.

Little did I know, I was making a data warehouse system and business intelligence before the concept existed. I have had several instances like that in my life where I was ahead of the market in the computer science world, but on the commercial side – because I wasn't a marketer or businessperson – I let the opportunity go just like that. Lesson learned: you can have all the technology in the world, but if you don't know how to market it and how to attract the right investors and how to do business and sell, you will never be successful.

I was finally able to graduate college in 1995. The Internet was brand-new, and the government realized that it was the new way of doing business and that it was going to be the base of a new economy. So, the government created an MBA program for computer science graduates that was completely customized. It was a one-year intensive program designed to teach marketing, sales, human resources, and accounting to computer science grads, so they could go out on their own and start businesses. As soon as I graduated, I applied for the program. The deal was that if you graduated from the program, it was paid for by the government and on top of that, the government would back up a business loan from the Royal Bank where if the business failed, the government would pay for the loan. It was 10,000 dollars. This was back in the 90s, so that would equate to about 30,000 dollars of today's money.

I went through the course, met some amazing friends, and I learned a lot. I was already fulfilling my desire of opening up my own business. I graduated, got my $10,000, and I had multiple ideas on what kind of business I wanted to open.

This was going to be my first start-up. I had a wife, a four-year-old kid, and a one-year-old baby. At the age of 25, I was fresh out of my second round of college. Was I ready to take the risky leap into the world of business?

# 3

# My very First Start-Up

*After college*

"The difference between a successful person and others is not a lack of strength, not a lack of knowledge, but rather, a lack in will."

– Vince Lombardi Jr.

Here I am, Mr. David Mansilla, 25 years old, with $10,000 in my bank account. It was the kind of money I had never seen before in my life. But it wasn't totally mine. It was a loan from the bank. I had the business acumen and some funding. What do I do now? Let's start my own business!

I had multiple ways I thought I could create revenue. Back then, they had just invented the first flat-bed scanners where you could digitize images, and the Internet was beginning to take off. I saw all these paper catalogues and fliers and I got the idea to buy the best camera and scanner I could find and go door-to-door to all the retail stores to see if I could make their catalogue *online.*

Basically, what I wanted to do was the first notions of e-commerce. I went and spent more than half of the money on this amazing digital equipment, and I went door-to-door for about three months trying to sell digital catalogues or websites. Everybody had no idea what the hell the Internet was, let alone a webpage. Needless to say, I didn't sell a single contract from this. I wasted the money buying all this fancy equipment without having the clients first. Another lesson learned: **you have to create the demand first before you invest in whatever it is you're trying to sell.** I did it backwards and it backfired on me. Now I only had $4,000 in the bank. I rented a small room above a retail store as my office and it put me back only $200 a month. The next idea I had was to write software the way I was doing for my brother.

When I started trying to become a software consultant, people wouldn't trust me with their projects because they considered me to be a junior software developer, even though I already had a system in place. Again, I was trying to knock on doors seeing how I could become a software consultant, and no one would hire me because I was a junior developer in their eyes. So, I started to panic as money began to run out. I didn't know what I was going to do, but I knew there had to be a way to make money with computers.

I called up a friend who was an electronics engineer, and he was very invested in hardware, including networking and personal computers. He trained me to build hardware and networks, and I ended up trying to sell them. I placed a small ad in the paper with the price set at 5% cheaper than the competition, and the first week I sold two computers. I was so happy! I was making about $100 per computer, which was amazing because it was the first time, I was making money with a business venture. I placed the ad again; I over-delighted my clients, and before I realized, I was selling ten computers a week. That quickly jumped to a hundred a week. I had to hire others to help me out, and I hired my dad as a contractor to help me set up a good assembly line. I was able to spend a year and a half selling all these computers.

In the end, however, I was kind of sad. It was a lot of work, it wasn't my passion, and I was in hardware when I wanted to be writing software. Thank God my brother kept the contract with me. I kept improving the Point of Sale system. I was still knocking on doors trying to sell software services. The problem was that during the time I was selling computers, I was giving a one-year warranty to the customers. People started knocking on my door because I was using cheap Chinese computer parts in order to be able to give the discounted price I was giving my clients. My manufacturers were great – they would replace the parts for me no problem. But I was getting more and more repairs, so I had to go to Toronto, get the parts, and spend the labor costs fixing the computers. I was only making 4-6% on them. The small amount I made the year before I was now spending on repairs. It wasn't all of the computers; it was only about 10% that came back. But just that little difference started to make a big hole in my bank account, to the point where I started struggling to make payroll. I had to let some people go and fix the computers myself. After a while, my wife reminded me that she had been holding down the fort in terms of bringing money in to support the family. I had been out of school for a year and a half and it was time for me to find something more stable for the sake of my wife and kids. I thought, "Oh my God, what do I do?" I had this software I built for my brother and I had about 1000 clients I sold computers to.

The summer before, I had sold a computer to an 18-year-old kid. He came to me and asked to intern with me. He told me that if I would teach him how to build computers, he would help me out free of charge. I agreed, and he worked for me the whole summer. He became one of my best employees! When I started to feel the squeeze, and I had to keep paying rent and paying back the loan, I thought I would have to close the business or go bankrupt. I had no idea what I was going to do.

Exactly a week after I thought I'd need to find an alternative option this kid comes back with his dad and a check book. They said, "David, we want to buy your business." I couldn't believe it. By then, my $10,000 debt was $20,000, and his father asked me how many clients I had. He asked me a few questions to check on the health of the business. After I answered all his questions, he asked me how much I wanted for the business. I said, "How about $20,000"? Done deal! He wrote me the check, and the business was his. The only thing I didn't sell him was the company name, because that was my reputation, and I would not include the Point of Sale software that I had been building. The first company I made was called Canada Digital Systems, Cadisys for short. It worked out great for everyone, since he had the cash flow needed to grow the company and to demand better prices from the suppliers. I actually checked five years later, and they were still thriving. We became long-time friends after that.

It's funny, though, because I realize now that I could have sold the business for $100,000, because I had a big client list and a great reputation. But I was desperate, and I didn't know anything about business. Even with just those $20,000, I paid my debt to the government, I paid off my credit cards, and I had a bit of time to find a real job. My brother was paying me a little bit to keep maintaining the software, which I worked on at night.

Little did I know, finding a job back in '96 was a real hustle. In today's world, software developers get a job the next day anywhere they want, if they're good. Back then, it was really difficult because it was like an engineering job. Companies didn't need that many developers yet.

## Golden Nuggets

- You have to **create demand** first before you invest in whatever it is you're trying to sell.
- Don't sell yourself short; find someone with more experience and talk over big decisions with them. They will be able to offer you clarity on how to **get the best outcome** from a situation.

# 4

# Corporate Rat Race

*Catching up with reality: The jump to my corporate rat race.*

"The pessimist sees difficulty in every opportunity. The optimist sees opportunity in every difficulty."

– Winston Churchill

The company was sold, my debts were paid off, and now I needed to find a place to work. I had to go hunting for a job. As it turned out, I read a book about finding a job and it said I needed to send out *at least* 100 resumes, and from those 100 few will call me in for an interview, and of those few, maybe one or two will offer me the position. This, I now know, is a lead generation campaign. I sent my first ten resumes, and nothing. I needed to make my resume more attractive. Along with the books on how to write the best resumes, I also got CD's that had information on how to do the interviews as well. I sent out more than 300 resumes over the period of three months. Of those, I got 5 interviews. Out of those 5, I was able to get one job offer. That was my first ever lead generation and sales effort that I did from scratch on a small scale. It took me ten years to realize that

I was actually *selling myself*! I didn't realize it then, but this is a major skill that I'd need to run a business.

Back then, it was all snail mail. I'd print out my resume, pack it in an envelope, and send it on its way. Then, I'd have to correspond with the HR manager of whoever was interested in bringing me in for an interview. I had to do this process so many times, which is something that would only take a few minutes now. I got several interviews, but I never got a call back. Until finally, I got three interviews, and one job offer. This was an exciting one. It was to be a junior developer at a national retailer, but they didn't offer me the job properly. They didn't make the decision on time. One of the other interviews was for the Waterloo Board of Education, and they called me in for a second interview. One of the most important things in life is to be prepared for whatever may come to you, even if it's unneeded in the end. In the second interview, I thought maybe there would be more than one person running it. I did more research on how to handle an interview with more than two or three interviewers at once. When I got to the second one, there were *four people* waiting for me in the room. There was the director of software development, the VP of IT, the HR manager, and the finance manager all in the same place looking back at me. I rocked the interview. Don't get me wrong – I was nervous, but the preparation paid off more than I could have imagined. One of the things that was crazy about this job was that they required the candidate to know about five computer languages. Of those five, I knew one. I was honest in my interview. I told them I only knew one, but that I'd pick up the rest as I went along. I already knew another five languages that they didn't require, and the logic for all of them was the same, so I at least had that backing me up. I then passed the technical test. I was hopeful. And then, silence.

I didn't hear from them for a while. 10 days go by, 15, all the while I'm still sending out resumes with the time crunch that comes with money running low. Finally, in mid-August, they call me up and ask me to come for one last interview. That last interview turned out to be my job offer! I became a junior developer for the Waterloo Board of Education. It was my first software developer job. The beautiful part of all this is that, if you think about it, you can always stretch yourself if you're honest with the person that is considering you for the job. You'll get a positive response if you show up with a great attitude and display your willingness to do whatever it takes to learn what your client needs to make them successful. When I got the job, I realized I wasn't considered a junior developer. They gave me an intermediate developer position. It was a blessing, because my salary scaled way more than I thought.

I put in 110% for this job, and I was so happy. I was the youngest person on the development team, but I was willing to learn and do whatever it took to stay ahead. I was bothering all my peers to teach me how to run the framework or how to do the operating system commands. To add extra value, I would stay two or three hours longer than everyone else because I was learning and wanted to show them that I'd do anything to supply the demands of the job. I came from a year and a half of losing money to gaining money every month. It was a blessing!

And although I was grateful for this, I still had that desire in my heart to run my own business.

When I sold the previous company, as you may remember, I kept my company name and the source code for my Point of Sale system. That was still mine, and so I still had hope to start my own thing again.

I quickly moved up the corporate ladder in that job. I started working with my boss and the head of development and he quickly realized that I was going to become better than anybody else because of the attitude I had. I was put on very critical projects thanks to that. After just three and a half months on the job, the other company, the national retailer, called and asked me to come for another job interview! They wanted me for the job, they were excited, and then... they were offering me $10,000 less than what I was getting at the Board of Education. Imagine if I would have waited for them. I would have gotten the job, but I would be back 10 grand and my future would have been completely different. This national retailer wanted me for my Point of Sale experience, the board of education hired me because of my attitude and willingness to learn, even though it was a completely different subject. Go after what you need. I needed to feed my family. Don't wait to see what happens. People wait for years and years and then they never do anything. You have to go get it.

I told my boss I got this offer, and he told me, "David, if they had offered you more, I would have counter-offered with more right away." This was only three months into the job. He then said, "You know how many people applied for this job?

Four-hundred people applied." In Canada, you get more than 80% of your salary when you retire if you get a government job like this. It also offers a lot of great benefits. It's a very stable industry to be in, so a lot of people wanted to work for them. I got selected out of 400 people, and he shared that with me because I told him about the other job interview. That's the power of *go get it,* and *don't take anything for granted.*

Until what you're looking for is already on your plate, you have to keep trying until you figure it out. **Don't be complacent.** These guys told me, *yeah, we're very interested and we'll call you back,* and they never did. They did it three months after I got another job.

I started growing at my corporate job with the Board of Education. I was learning faster; I was the only kid in the whole room. I learned how to drink coffee, and I quickly got to about seven or eight cups a day. I didn't realize until I noticed my hands shaking and decided I had to slow it down! About seven months into the job, they asked me to take care of all the school administration software. We had about 100 schools with over 2000 teachers and over 50,000 students. A board of education works like a corporation with franchises. You have the head office, and then you have all the schools. I was in charge of the software running on every single computer at the administrational level, and I was to write programs to make their lives easier. One of them was the special education program, and I poured my heart and soul into that system because it was to help kids that had special needs, and this was going to help their learning. I created this beautiful program, but I did it in conjunction with a lady that was super passionate about these kids. We got together, and we developed this amazing program. This lady was an office manager for one of the schools. I didn't realize it at the time, but she was going to be my first mentor on top of being one of my most important clients later on in life.

At the same time that I finished the Special Ed system, there was a big requirement from the government to have standardized reporting for the report cards. They started searching to see if local development teams from schoolboards could do it. This was a big provincial level project, not just at the board level. The director brought me in with my boss and they asked us, can you guys pull it off? Can we do it ourselves, or should we wait for the government to come up with something? I said, anything is possible. So, my boss said, "If David thinks we can do it, we can do it." I got assigned to the project. I had to do it on a Mac, because the school administration was running on Windows, but all the teacher's computers were running on Mac, and this was going to be a software for the teachers. So, I taught myself how to write on Mac. I remember I did it on something called Real Basic, which is a computer language similar to Visual Basic but for Mac, and I had to import databases and do all the crazy work. After this eight-month project, I had the provincial report card running smoothly across thousands of teachers and schools. Not only that, but we actually finished the system before the government officials finished theirs. In fact, we finished it about three years earlier. They started using us as a model for other school boards until the government could come up with a consulting firm that could write a system for the whole province.

My director took notice in me and started giving me a lot of the tools I needed to grow. A year later, I got my first gig. I got an inquiry from a company that needed a Point of Sale system. I couldn't believe it. I picked up the phone and they asked me if I still had the system. The only thing that I did to advertise my system was leave flyers at my brother's stores. It was very revolutionary because it was a computer running the sales, it wasn't a cash machine. So, somebody picked up this flier and called me! I had a meeting with them and told them Saturday's were all I had available because by then, I was working full time. When I realized these guys were serious, I called my boss. Again, **transparency and honesty will always help you win. The truth will set you free**. I never lied. I talked to my boss and told them that I had this opportunity to work on a Point of Sale system that I already had but that it was away from business hours. I told them it had nothing to do with the education system and all the things I was working on for them, and I asked if they would let me do it. They were completely happy with it, as long as I didn't work on that during business hours. They changed my contract to allow me to run this other contract at night.

I signed the contract with this new company, it was a big 10,000 sq. ft. store that was for hobbies and crafts, and the guy told me that he needed me to set up the entire network to put up five POS terminals and to have two servers in the back end. "I want to do labels and complete automation, and I want to do it all in Windows or Mac". My program was all text-based, and this guy wanted a Graphical User Interface program. I told him,

"Listen, I got this program right now and it works great. If you give me the chance, I can convert it into Windows no problem." I had never written a single Windows program in my life, however, by now I already had experience writing Mac software. I figured it wouldn't be so different. I stretched myself again! I was honest with him. I told him I needed to learn how to do it, and if he was willing to trust me, I would get it done for him. The guy said "I trust you. I've seen the system other stores use and they talk wonders about you." Of course, they did. It was my brother's store! Thank God he was very happy with me.

Here I am, embarking in my first professional job and at the same time at night, I had my first professional software development project *as a business!* I was completely happy, but I wasn't sure when I'd see my wife and kids. I would go to the school board from 8 to 5, I would run to see my wife and kids around 6pm, I would then drive half an hour to another city, and from 6pm to sometimes midnight I'd write the other Point of Sale system. It was fabulous. I was on fire.

I made a promise to my wife. **You always have to have a balance in your life otherwise you lose everything**. If you are single, go for it. But if you're married and you have kids like I did, you have to take care of your family, too. So, I made a pact with my wife that from Monday to Friday, I would always be working no matter what. Saturday and Sunday were always the time for the family. I would only work if there was a huge emergency. I implemented that after three months of not seeing my family. That promise saved my marriage. I'm happy to report that I'm about to celebrate being married for thirty years. Maybe when this book comes out, it will already have been thirty years. **It's possible to find success without sacrificing your family life.**

Two years into that job, my director left to work for the largest telecommunications company in the country. They were spinning off a new enterprise that would take care of the entire retail operations for the whole country. My old director called me one day, and he invited me out to this fancy hotel restaurant in downtown Toronto. He said, "David, I want you to come work for me." I replied, "With the salary that I have, plus the gasoline and travelling expenses, I'm gonna make less money if I do." He said, "What if I doubled your salary?" My immediate response: "Where do I sign?"

It was an amazing opportunity, but now I had to be driving one hour in the morning and an hour and a half to go home. I still had that contract running with the hobbies store in the evenings. I consulted with my wife, and we agreed that we would continue to respect our weekends. The city I worked in during the evenings was on the way back from Toronto anyway, so I could still keep up my night contract. My boss knew that I still had that. This new job was to be a senior architect for the new Point of Sale system for all the retail stores in this telecommunications company. It was a big deal. But again, the other store wasn't in competition because it had different needs.

So, I was hired. I was the guy that was doing whatever it took to delight my clients. I was the one saying yes to all the challenges. **Always go the extra mile, and you will always succeed.** Why? Because most people are complacent with what they want. That's fine if that's what they choose. But I was always thirsty for more and for adding massive value. I was grateful I got a job that was paying me, because I came from years of losing money, so the gratitude was ingrained in me. It wasn't because I was cocky or because I was trying to be the best. It was all my gratitude. If you keep that mentality, there is nothing but success for you. However, **you have to come from a humble and grateful place, not from an aggressive and arrogant position. You can still be successful like that, but you will never be fulfilled.**

After being offered the job and double the salary, I asked my old director if I could keep my part time gig. The hobbies store contract was going strong and I needed the extra income. If I didn't, even though they doubled my salary, I'd still be making a little bit less money than with my current salary plus my night gig. He said there was no problem.

The commute became pretty bad. My wife and I agreed this would work if we continued to respect weekends, and we did. When they doubled my salary, even putting into consideration the gas expense, and the vehicle depreciation, I was making at least 35% more money. In fact, this allowed me to buy my first house. We saved enough down payment for the house thanks to selling the first business, and as it turned out, we weren't filing the necessary deductions during the income tax years while the business was running. When we hired a professional accountant to review our income tax filings, he was able to get us back the down payment of our first house in taxes that we overpaid. This alone was a huge miracle and the catalyst of our first property. This also made it possible for my wife to stay home and go back to university. How amazing is that? It was my first experience in a big corporation. I was ready to jump with both feet in.

## Golden Nuggets

- **Transparency** and **honesty** will always help you win. The **truth** will set you free.
- It's possible to find **success without sacrificing** your family life.
- Always go the **extra mile** and you will succeed. Others are complacent with what they do. If you're thirsty for **adding massive value**, nothing can stop you.
- You have to come from a **humble** and **grateful** place, not from an aggressive and arrogant position. You can still be successful like that, but you will never be fulfilled.

# 5

# Finding Mentors

## *Welcome to professional consulting*

"A mentor is someone who allows you to see the hope inside yourself."

– Oprah Winfrey

I was now the senior architect of a new Point of Sale system project for a company that had presence across the country. This was huge. I felt excited and motivated. My old director became my new boss – I didn't have anybody in between and I had full freedom. Even though the company was a huge corporation, this section had only a thousand employees out of the 80,000 of the whole company. A thousand employees felt like a huge company for me, but it was small enough that the IT and software department was a tight group. We hired an outsourced team from Boston to do the coding in Java. I started on all the architecture with my Point of Sale experience I acquired through my own business.

I was hitting home run after home run. It was fantastic. I was putting all my effort into it, and I was being all I could be. Sometimes I even had to skip my side gig to stay overnight, because we'd have to prevent things going wrong with the build or with the production environment. Sometimes we'd have to go visit the stores to make sure the Point of Sale system was working correctly. At that job, the person sitting next to me happened to have his own business with five employees. He was working there on a contract through his company. He wasn't a full-time employee like I was. We started to catch on. He was about 15 years older than me. He was an amazing guy, drove a great car, and his energy was fantastic. What a great example of a true consultant, a true software and infrastructure consultant. He told me, "You know what David, let's go play squash". I had never played squash in my life before. He told he'd teach me. For lunch, instead of eating out, we'd go to the gym and we'd hit the ball for forty-five minutes to an hour. I got very proficient in squash. I could make points. He was so good at squash that he could win matches against me with his left hand, and he was right-handed! Even after a year, this stayed true.

The most amazing part, however, was that he became my first true mentor in life. He told me why I was doing what I was doing, and I told him I already had a side business that I take care of at night. He said, "David, you're cutting yourself short. You have to make the jump and go full time on contracting. You're going to make more money, and you'll have the chance to expand." But then, I asked him, "what about the bonuses and the vacations and all the benefits?" He said, "Yeah, I guess you don't have that, and you don't get the security. But at the end of the day, you're the owner of your own time, you're your own boss, and you have a greater chance to become financially independent." So, we kept talking and talking. Eventually, he started giving me examples of people like him who were more like my age (I was almost thirty by then). He was a pivotal person in my life at that time.

We became really good friends, but I didn't have the guts to quit my job because my wife was in school, we had kids, and I already had my side gig. I needed to feel the security of a full-time job. On top of that, the trauma from the first business that I happened to sell was still very fresh in my mind. So, I decided to keep learning the lessons he was telling me, but I didn't execute anything. I just started to make the best of the jobs I had.

When I was going through Bell – now that I said it, it's Bell, what the hell – I started noticing they were hiring a lot of contractors from other companies. Especially this company called CGI. They were charging a lot of money for services that I was doing three-fold. My boss came to me at one point and said "David, every time we have a new build in the stores for a new version of the software, we have to spend $100,000." This was because they had to send a team to every store to do the installments, and it racks up the costs. He asked me, "Can you figure something out, so we at least cut that in half?" And of course, I replied with, "Leave it to me." I mulled it over for about a week and thought, *Okay, what if I architect a program that allows us to have a small client at every store? I designate a computer as the host, and then this computer will connect to the server overnight, when no one is using the computers, and connect to the server at the head office. It'll check to see if there's a new update just by flipping a switch in a file.* This was the simplest solution I could think of.

I decided to show him the plan. I had to write low-level TCPIP calls (Transmission Control/Internet Protocol) to get the load because the java files were huge. Sometimes, it even required a java library update. I showed the design to my boss and I asked them for a budget to see if we could actually get this done, and he gave me the green light! It took me about a month to build the first prototype. We tried it with one of the stores. Basically, the store's main computer would wake up every night at midnight and it would check to see if there was an update or file. Then it would connect to the server and the server would confirm an update and it would load it overnight. It would take like four hours to download because it was really big, and the Internet was very slow. Once the download was ready, it would automatically install the update locally at the store and then the rest of the computers would connect to the main computer, grab the installer files and automatically install the software everywhere. By the time the people at the store level would come in, the software would have been updated. This was the year 2000. It worked perfectly in one store and my boss said "Okay, let's try five stores." Before we knew it, we were running hundreds of stores. The funny thing is, I didn't even have to hire a development team. I had enough passion to do it all myself. I dedicated myself to doing it and saved the company $100,000 per update. Sometimes we were doing builds twice or three times a month! So, that's like $3-400,000 a month just in savings. They were just amazed. They celebrated me. Recognition felt great.

Back on my side gig, I was finishing up the Graphical User Interface for them and my client was super happy. The sales were through the roof. He said, "How about if we put barcode systems and automatic inventory ordering with purchase orders?" And I said, "No problem!" That took me about four months to implement and before I knew it, his warehouse was working like a UPS or FedEx. It was fantastic. Needless to say, he was very happy.

While this was happening with the store and for Bell Canada, someone else reached out to me with a new opportunity. Remember the lady I was writing the special education software with? She was the school manager. She gives me a call and says, "David! I need your help! I just quit my job and I need a bunch of programming done for this new system that I'm building. I realized that we were processing thousands and thousands of dollars a day at the school level, and there's no software for it! We tried Excel, Quicken, and everything we try is breaking. The board didn't want to spend the money to have an accounting system that was distributed." They ended up doing all the cash accounting manually. It was a pain in the ass! She told me, "I have this passion. I want to see the school administrators cutting their time back to 2 hours or less instead of the 9 a day it takes to account for all the money. Can you help me out? I know you have your side gig." I was so excited, but where would I get the time to do this? We went for coffee and I expressed my gratitude towards her. I told her I could help her out but that I wouldn't be able to help with the main development, because I knew she was capable of taking the brunt. She needed help mostly with the low-level programming, the installations, the file transfers, the connectivity to the Internet, automation, all that. I said that I'd only work on the utilities to make her life easier. Then, what I could do was dedicate one day a week for her. I negotiated with my other side gig and said instead of working five days a week, I'd work four. Also, there was another school manager from a different school, and they both partnered on this venture. They were both very proficient at writing software in a local database system.

The relationship with her started growing. She's one of the most positive people in my life, and we kept on building together. I broke the rules a little bit because sometimes I'd go on Saturday mornings to her house to dialogue what the next build was going to look like. But it was never more than one or two hours. Thank God she's an early morning person – she wakes up at 4 am every day. So, we'd meet at 6am and then by the time I was back in the house, my family was about to wake up. This way, I didn't steal any time from them or from my wife. I had to remember the rules. There's no money in the world that can replace fulfillment, and having a beautiful family is part of that fulfillment.

She started injecting a lot of positivity in my life. She had this attitude where anything was possible if you have enough passion and enough reason to achieve it. She inspired me so much. She had quit her job, and her little company started to grow! The services that I rendered to her started to grow, too. I had to hire a contractor that could help me out because my time was completely full.

Everything was going great, but then... something started happening to me. Remember how I was completely humble in my first job? I came from losing money every month, and that made me so happy that I was doing ten times more than everybody else. A little bit of change started to happen in my soul and in my mind, and I didn't realize it was going on. This feeling was very sneaky. I started going from gratitude to expectation, and I especially started to feel it when I found out how much money Bell was paying their contractors. I started to feel this deep change in my attitude.

A little monster started to grow inside me. Since I didn't know better, I started to feed it. Things were beginning to go downhill.

## Golden Nuggets

- **Mentors show you what is possible**. They expand your mind and help you dream bigger. Our scope of possibility starts off so small until you talk to someone who's done what you thought was the impossible.
- The minute you start realizing that you can count on other people's time and intellect, you begin to build a real business – not only self-employment.

# 6

# Staying Humble

*Stay humble or get humbled by life.*

"True humility is not thinking less of yourself;
it is thinking of yourself less."
– Rick Warren

It was October, and I had just implemented the automated software installation system across Canada. I had changed my itinerary so that I could accommodate my mentor, Kim, for her new school accounting program. As always, I was also doing the Point of Sale system for the hobbies store. These were the state of things when my problem began to show.

I think a big part of my change in attitude was not only the amount of money I found out the contractors were getting paid at Bell, but I began to see the wear and tear of driving. By this time, I had been commuting for about two years already. It was really tearing me apart. I didn't have enough time to relax – I was always on the go. I was a young person, but it eventually started to take a hold of me. Then, I realized that some of those contractor guys were getting paid so much because some of them were billing up to four times what I was getting paid. When I did the math,

I realized I wasn't even making half of that with my full-time job. So, I got angry. I turned my appreciation into expectation. I went to talk to my boss, and I asked him for a raise. I told him I saved at least $400,000 a month with the program I made them, and these other guys were being paid more. I said I deserved more. Imagine, *deserved.* And they had already doubled my salary when they hired me. On top of that, my bonus was 15%. I was making a killing with the bonuses at the end of the year! While I did that, I knew I needed a break, so I thought of finding a job back home. All I did was put my resume on Monster or Workopolis, and sure enough I'd get ten or fifteen people calling to inquire for me. Remember, this was just before the .com crash. That didn't affect Canada too much, so we were still in need of developers.

My boss came back, and he said that they wouldn't be able to give me a pay increase until the next year. It was October and I'd have to wait until January to even just talk about it. Meanwhile, a new job offer came through. They wouldn't be able to match the salary, but it was in town. They said I'd be so happy there. They made it seem like the team would treat me like family, so I went to all the interviews. They warned me that there were some issues with the parking, but as an incentive they said they'd give me a parking spot right in front of the building. I was moving to another huge corporation, but in this case, the corporation didn't have a smaller corporation inside like they did at Bell. This one was huge, and it was all over the place. It was one of the largest insurance companies in the country. It was a blessing by the way, because from learning telecommunications systems, I was now learning insurance. Both eventually became experiences that helped me in my future business ventures.

I gave my resignation to my boss. Keep in mind, my boss was almost like a friend to me. I told him, "I found another job. I can't commute this far anymore." I was going to be paid a little less, but I'd be saving in gas and time in traffic. My boss asked, "Can you please wait until January? If you wait until then, you'll get to cash your bonus, and I can try to raise your salary as much as I can. I need you right now."

You know, it would have been so easy for me to talk to the head-hunter and say, *I'll take the job, but I'll take it in January.* But I was so arrogant and proud. Instead, I told him I was leaving in 10 days because I thought he didn't deserve me. My boss took me out for dinner because he knew that I had a beautiful soul and that I was just overreacting. He said, "David, it's okay that you're leaving. You're leaving a lot of money on the table for being impatient and refusing to wait a couple of months. I wish you the best, but remember, it doesn't matter how good you are because there is always someone better than you. The minute that you stop being humble and start feeding your pride, you trigger your ego and that can kill you." He told me he loved me and that he wished me the best. That was the last time we ever spoke.

I now had a new job. My side gigs were blossoming. Thank God I didn't get overly proud in my side gigs. I was always humble with them and it was great. It was my passion! I really wanted to have my own business, but I couldn't jump into that alone! In my mind, I couldn't, because I didn't want to risk it.

It was time to enter this giant insurance company. Three months into the job, I realized that the parking was only a three-month deal that I didn't know about. It was in the contract, but I didn't read it. I just signed it. After the time was up, I had to find a parking spot that was about a kilometer away. I had to walk through the snow every morning and every evening. Can you imagine? I'm a Latin tropical guy walking through the snow for ten blocks every single day to get to the office! Oh man, I was so mad. I was so mad! And then, to make matters worse, making a tiny change in the software that I was managing required multiple meetings and architecture reviews. There were all these hoops to jump through. Changing the location of a small button required about a month of meetings and planning. The company was so big, and the software was so stable that it made this process necessary.

Of course, I ended up getting bored. I started trying to find inside projects where I could make a big difference. I started to increase my productivity with my team. A good thing about the job change is that I became a development manager. I was moving up the corporate ladder. I became a development leader with a team of twelve people. It was kind of the same as with Bell, but Bell was through contractors in Boston and in Toronto. The difference with this new position was that everyone was here and worked for me in the same office.

I started scavenging for little projects that I could have full freedom on because working on the corporate applications was a pain in the ass! It was way too slow for me. Through making connections and selling myself, I was finally able to connect with another department that was in charge of the software licensing. It was awesome. We ran it like a start-up company. We had to do thousands of software assessments on every single PC. They had people all over the place and they even had people outside of Canada. I had to envision a software that could go in, read the registry, bring the database back and make sure every single license was legal. If it was illegal it would take inventory of how much illegal software was installed, whether it was compatible with the corporations or not, and if it was, to pay the license before we got audited. We were doing so much good work in there. My team got super motivated and I really felt what it was like to be in a start-up for the first time. I managed to create my own little start-up within this humungous corporation.

The project was a complete success. We delivered online reporting through the web. Managers could see their own staff and what they installed in the computer, what was right, and what was wrong. I used the same methodology I was using for the software update back in my last job. I was sending little systems that installed themselves and they would actually read all the data in the computer and in the registry, report back to the central server with what happened, and then create a web report for all the final reporting and analytics.

That saved me. I was about to leave that job because I felt useless. **There is nothing worse in life than feeling useless, no matter how much money you make.** Material possessions will give you pleasure, which is in the body. Making money will tell your mind that it's secure, which is bullshit, but the sense of security will make you happy. But nothing will make you more fulfilled in your soul than knowing that whatever you are doing is adding value to the world. That's why I was miserable those first six or seven months in this new job! Moving one button from one place to another and having that simple change take a month to get done made me feel like I wasn't adding value. I felt like I was just collecting my salary.

As soon as I lost my parking spot, that was when I realized God was teaching me a lesson. I started to realize that I had become proud. I started to practice gratitude again. Every time I walked through the cold to get to work, I didn't care. I was getting what I deserved. And then, I started doing the math! All the thousands of dollars left on the table, all the reputation that I ruined and all the bridges I burned because I didn't wait two more months at my old job. Oh my God! And maybe they would have given me a raise because I was ready for a promotion. All this because I was too proud to wait two months. Every time I walked through the snow, freezing my ass off, I was thinking about all these thousands and thousands of dollars, how I could have taken my family to Disney and back, or maybe even a cruise. Instead of that, I was walking in the snow to get to a job where nobody cared if I did it or not.

The biggest lesson, however, came later. About a year and a half into that job, they had a big announcement that there was an even bigger insurance company that was going to buy all the stocks in the company. As a result, they were going to lose thousands of jobs because they became redundant. They told people to get ready because there were going to be early retirements and they'd be giving packages to people that need to leave.

I needed a fulltime job because my wife was going through school and she was full time at home, too. She was taking care of the kids and going to school in the evenings. I was paying a mortgage. I wasn't making enough money part-time on my side gigs to cover it all. I felt completely threatened by this news. If they let me go, I feared I wouldn't be able to pay my mortgage and I'd lose the house. I started proactively looking for another job, and still, the humility came back. How stupid was I? Why did I quit my last job so early? I should have kept it! But I got proud. I learned to be humble the hard way.

When I started looking for a job, I was completely surprised. I started looking for jobs locally, but I couldn't find anything that paid what I was already making. That forced me to look in Toronto again. Back to the miserable commute. I had about three or four head-hunters helping me. We were going through all these possibilities together, but I had to have a job with enough flexibility that would allow me to work on my side gig. I also needed to grow as a person professionally.

And then, a miracle happened.

I got my next job.

## Golden Nuggets

- Having **expectations** instead of **appreciation** is the fastest way to lead an unfulfilled life.
- Do whatever you can to end relationships on good terms. All we have in our jobs and businesses is the **connections we make**.
- Realizing you made a mistake is the first step towards your personal growth.
- Use your consequences to reflect on how to make better choices in the future.

# 7

# Risking it All

*A wife, three kids, and a mortgage. Let's quit my nice management job and go full-time in the software services arena.*

"Dissatisfaction is a great starting point, for it is right there that we have the most power, strength, and energy to push change through."

– David DeNotaris

The job interview I went to was really strange. Instead of going to an office, the VP of Development gave me a lunch appointment. I didn't know that it was a strategy at the time, but he had invited me out to see how I would respond in a social environment. I was a little nervous when I went. At this point, I was also completely humble. This job offer was for the largest lab testing facility in Canada. They had coast-to-coast presence, but it was run like a family business because it *was* a family business. They came together as mergers with other smaller laboratories until they became a big conglomerate.

The company needed somebody to lead the development team that was scattered across the country. Now, we're talking

2003, so the Internet was still pretty slow. It would definitely be a challenge to handle such a unique situation. My boss found something in me that made him believe that I could do it. He wanted to lead a database migration project. The one they were currently using was weak, and they wanted to transition to one that would better suit their needs. They had to find a new Director of Development to be in charge of the growing team. This wasn't a small project; this was a multi-million-dollar effort, so there was a lot at stake. The VP hired me right on the spot. He noticed that I had the drive to do it. Again, I was transparent about my side gigs and there was no conflict, so it worked out perfectly.

I didn't realize it right away, but I had embarked on one of the most difficult projects of my life. The laboratory was great, and my boss became one of my best mentors. He taught me how to travel, how to hire people remotely and how to speak the subtle language of different cultures. We would go to Montreal, Quebec, the West coast, and East coast. Everybody behaved differently and had their own cultures. And there we'd be, two guys from Toronto. Everyone would look at us like we were arrogant people because we were Torontonians. It wasn't the case! In fact, I had learned my lesson, so I was very humble. I quickly started to improve the reputation of the development team, and I started hiring rock-stars. Before I knew it, we had a large team and we were right into the project. This project was incredibly hard to accomplish, but we finished it on time despite the challenges. The budget was respected as well. Once we finished this part of the project, the ownership of the company gained enough confidence in us to keep building the laboratory management system so that they could manage all the different disciplines. This was a large lab, so they would do food, environmental, water, and DNA testing, and whatever else was needed in the industry. We embarked on this project, moving from one technology to another. This was after the database movement.

The company kept getting mergers and acquisitions and every time we would compete with another company to merge, the first thing that they needed to decide was what laboratory information management system (LIMS) they were going to use. Our system would always win because it was the most robust, but I had to convince the executives on why our system was better. I did this by being honest and analyzing the other systems to see if ours wasn't the best. I always came out on top and that gave me a huge lesson on how to negotiate, sell and present at a corporate level. I think God gave me this company as a steppingstone for my own business. It taught me everything I needed to know before I knew I needed it. I was going to have developers in other countries in the future. I already knew how to travel and how to manage requests from multiple offices across the country.

By the time this happened, the store I had for the Point of Sale system started to wind down a little bit. I was only doing a couple of days a week there, but the school cash system started to grow! I started to build and build, and at one point they wanted to move to the web. I developed the entire architecture to move this product to the web. You know what I did?

I took a month-long vacation from my full-time job and I spent the entire month building the architecture with one of my best friends.

I hired him as a contractor. I remember we took our families out of the country. He took his family to Europe where he was from, and I took my family and sent them to Disney. The entire month, we lived together in his apartment in downtown Toronto and we would code for 13-14 hours straight. We would go down at 3 AM to have Greek food because we were in Greek town. It was fantastic. Within a month, we finished the first iteration of the architecture needed to move the school accounting system to the cloud. It was incredibly inspiring. I remember thinking, *this is what I was born to do.*

Little by little, I was getting more attracted to taking the big leap and starting my own business. This is the lesson. Here is the golden nugget. **If you know what you want and are willing to do whatever it takes to get it, you will always get it.** I will give you a real example. The year that I got hired as the Director of Development for the laboratory company, I met one of the developers and we became really good friends. He was the best guy I had around. I started teaching him the leadership skills I had accumulated along the way; he was like my sidekick. One day, I asked my boss when he started working at the company. He told me he started working there a year ago. I told him I saw his profile, and his employment history said that he had only been there for two months. My boss replied, "Yeah, you know why? He volunteered for an entire year to work here." *What?! He didn't get paid for a whole year!?*

He was a volunteer for the entire year because they had no developer positions available at the time he applied. He needed the experience because he was from Romania and was starting new. He insisted so much that they had to talk to HR to make sure they were protected legally so he could do an internship with them. After a year, the opportunity came and of course, he became a full-time employee and he was one of the most grateful employees and developers that they had. Imagine that! Are you willing to work for free for one year to get what you want? **The problem isn't that a goal is impossible to achieve. It's that we're not willing to do what it takes to have what we want.** There is a big difference in that. Often times, it takes doing something that no one else is willing to do.

When I saw that the LIMS system was already in place, my boss told me to choose someone from my team to train and pass along all my knowledge to, so they had back up in case I left. When he said that, something clicked in my heart. I thought, *you know what, it's time to start moving towards having my own business.*

Guess who I picked to take my place? I picked the guy that volunteered. His name was Sorin, and I picked him because he had the best attitude, the most humility, and he was the guy that did whatever it took. I trained him on how to be an amazing manager and leader, and I put him in the position to replace me.

I gave my resignation to my boss. I told him "I love you, and thank you, but I need to start doing my own thing." My boss told me, "No problem, David, just make sure this guy is well trained." I had learned my lesson. I stayed for another three or four months to make sure Sorin was running okay, and once I knew that he didn't need me, I got another job. I knew this was going to be my last job.

The head office of this new company was back in town where I lived. It had 75 people and they were selling half a billion dollars a year, but it was a franchise model. They had retail stores all over the country, but the people that actually managed the corporation was a group of just 75. The IT department consisted of about ten people. I was hired to lead their department, specifically on the software side, to update them into modern technologies. They were still running with 90s tech! I knew it was going to be an easier job because of the size of the team.

In my job interview, I was honest as always and told them I had a part time business. I told them I wanted to take this on and make the company amazing. Once I knew everything was working fine, I could hire my replacement and go full time on business. I was honest from the very beginning. Totally transparent. I got hired and I actually took a 30% pay cut, but it was okay because it was my steppingstone. My wife was about to graduate from computer science, too, so it was only a matter of time until she'd get a job and pass the probation. If she got a full-time job, she could pay the basic bills, and I'd have enough resources to find some clients and be on my own, which was the dream. I ended up working in this company for a year and a half. I became very good friends with the owner and VP of Finance and Technology. It was great. It was a beautiful job. They treated me like royalty. Since it was a prosperous company, they would give us breakfast and lunch, and they'd mark it down as if we were testing the items and, in a way, we *were* testing them. My life got back in balance because the workload was heavy, but it was manageable. It wasn't like the three jobs that I had before. I started to grow more and more on my business as a contractor on the school company, and the Point of Sale system company was getting slower and slower. It was perfect. After my time there, I was ready to jump.

The owner of this company was a multi-millionaire. His cottage has an 18-hole golf course and is located in one of the best places in Northern Ontario called the Muskoka's. He actually asked me for lunch, and we went. He told me, "David, I wanted to take you to lunch because what you're doing is brave and I wanted to give you one piece of advice. Just one. Bill on time."

"What do you mean?"

"Most of my friends that went into their own businesses went bankrupt because they never sent the bill on time and they never asked for their money. You control the rules. Not your clients. Your clients will be willing to do what you want them to as long as you are exceptional. Not excellent, **exceptional.** Outstanding. If you're outstanding, you can set your own rules. My advice is, bill weekly and do net 10. Don't do net 30. Do net 10."

Guess what? I took that advice so seriously that even today, that's where my billing is at right now and this has saved our butts in the company so many times. Our cash flow is fairly healthy because of that. Even when some clients fall behind, because the rest of the clients are paying on time, we have no problem. So, always take the advice of your mentors seriously and apply them because knowledge is not power. **Applied knowledge is power**. Tony Robbins says it all the time. It's not what you know. It's how you use what you know that matters. I'm gonna give you another example from another lunch.

When I was growing out of Maxxam Analytics, the President of the company, Pierre, took me out for lunch, too. He knew that I was leaving because I wanted to start my own business. He knew I was taking a short-term job until I figured it out. Pierre gave me some advice that to this day, most of my net worth is thanks to this. Pierre told me, "David, from now on, whatever you do in life, try to become a shareholder. Always try to become a shareholder for two reasons: number one, when you become a shareholder, you are showing the client that you care so much that you're willing to go bankrupt if they go bankrupt. They will know that you're willing to do whatever it takes to make them successful. Two: if the company goes up in value, partly because of your work and theirs, that's how you become a millionaire. As an investor – not as an employee or a worker. You become a millionaire as an investor." I really took this to heart. I didn't understand this back then because I knew nothing about investing, but it was in the back of my head.

It was finally time for me to step up to the plate. I remember it was summer, July 2005. I was shaking. My wife already had a job and had it for over seven months at this point. She was getting regular pay. I was talking to my friends and mentors asking, "Is it time? Is it time to quit my big beautiful safety net and go full time on business?"

They said, "If you don't do it now, David, you will never do it." Especially my mentor, Kim. She told me, "David, I could actually even use more of your hours if you quit. But I don't have the money to pay you, but I could use your hours!" She said, "Go ahead!"

I had a big meeting with my wife. I said, "Mi Amor, are you ready?" She confirmed we were ready. I actually quit the job and I didn't have a new contract. I was still just entertaining the school software at night and by then, the store where I was doing the Point of Sale system got sold, effectively cancelling my contract. I only had the small amount of income that I was getting from the school cash system and consulting, and nothing else. I started panicking. I was going to be out of the job by the end of August. I was incredibly nervous. What was I going to do? I had no money saved because every penny I made had to go to family expenses and taxes. It was a true leap of faith.

I started looking for opportunities as a full-time contractor, and I was blessed enough to have lunch with somebody whose business was finding technology contracts for people like me, for contractors who were by themselves and who wanted to charge per hour as a corporation instead of being a full-time employee. By now, the employment for software developers, architects, and project management leaders was very high because there was even more technology coming about. People were demanding a lot of these types of positions. Where I live, we have the biggest Startup community in Canada, so it was perfect. Everything lined up. To make the long story short, two days after officially leaving my job, I landed my first contract as a company, as ISU Corp (www.isucorp.ca). It was only a two-month contract, so I was still pretty scared despite having a new project. That meant that I was going to make enough money to meet all my financial responsibilities instead of going into debt.

By the way, to open the new company, I decided to grab $300 from a little consulting gig and that's what I was going to use to open the bank account for the corporation. I didn't want to loan money like before. It was going to be completely bootstrapped by me. Nobody else's money was going to be used. To this day, that's still how we run this company. We haven't had a single dime of external money as an investment or loan, with the exception of smart loans for property investing, but we'll learn about that in later chapters.

## Golden Nuggets

- **If you know what you want and are willing to do whatever it takes to get it, you will always get it.**
- If you're waiting for the right time to jump into the business, it will never be the right time. You could try to manage to catch a wave in the market, but it goes up and down all the time. If you wait and wait, you will probably never do it. Courage is doing what you need to do despite the fear you have. It's okay to be afraid but be courageous and do it anyway.
- Don't borrow money if you don't need it. Don't use somebody else's money if you do not need it. However, if you need it, borrow it because borrowing money when you need it and when you have it is easier than trying to borrow it when you **really** need it. When you really need money, nobody will want to lend it to you. When you're okay financially, you can negotiate better with the bank and they'll give you a line of credit, or an economic lease you can use when you're in trouble.
- Knowledge isn't power. **Applied knowledge** is power.

# 8

# Delegate or Die

*One of the most difficult choices I have ever made – uninstalling my compilers and letting everyone else write all the code.*

"An entrepreneur is someone who will jump off a cliff and assemble an airplane on the way down."

— Reid Hoffman

Here I was, in the first two months of my new contract. The company only wanted to have me there for two months because the program was so complicated that they didn't want to engage in a longer-term contract if they didn't know that the technology was going to work. Basically, these guys were writing software for MFPs, which is a fancy way of saying smart photo copiers. They didn't even know how to turn this machine on. I was in charge of the Sharp version of the sophisticated machine. These machines were so big that they probably took half the size of a small room. They had a computer embedded in it. My job was to figure out how the machine worked, figure out the operating system underneath, and see how I could connect the software of the backend system that was written for enterprise automation.

To me, it was a huge challenge. I didn't even know where to start. I grabbed the manual, I figured out how to turn it on within a couple of hours. Then I downloaded a simulator from the website of the operating system and started learning it. Within 15 days, I had written documentation on how to operate the machine from the software perspective. Then, I started negotiating with the people from Japan, and with the people there that engineered the photo copier. We began to see how we could connect to the backend software and what software I needed to write. It was one of the most challenging things I ever did in my life. The Japanese engineers didn't have enough English knowledge and English wasn't my first language either! We couldn't communicate! However, we made a lot of progress and at the end of the first month, I demonstrated to my first client that it was something we could actually use. We could write software to take advantage of the backend software that they had which is what they wanted in order to use this model of photocopier for their clients. My client still wasn't convinced, so he said, "Listen, your corporate contract is expired in thirty days. Do a prototype and if it works after thirty days, then we'll think about extending your contract."

It was time for me to get some help. I was working thirteen hours a day on this project. I was only dedicating eight to ten hours a week to the school system. I talked to them and I told them my situation, and they knew I needed to make the revenue to stay in business. It worked out because they were a little strapped on money anyways, so it was a win-win for everybody. By now I didn't have the contract in the retail Point of Sale system, so I could focus 100% on this new contract. But I needed help. One of the reasons why I decided to go into business was because in my corporate jobs, every time I wanted to hire somebody like an amazing developer, they'd be gone within a year because they were paying more money somewhere else. It was that, or they'd leave because the culture wasn't right, and I didn't know what culture was back then. I was losing all these people all the time.

I had a strategy in my mind to fix this. As you know, my first computer science degree came from back home, Guatemala, and I considered myself a good developer. I always had it in the back of my mind to go to other countries that have the same time zone and hire exceptional developers. None of my employers allowed me to do it. I had a theory that this could be done. Now that I had my own business, I needed help, and I went and did it.

I put an ad up online. The only thing that I didn't want was to not be able to work the same hours. My logic said I didn't want people more than a three-hour time zone difference. I still want to be able to work eight hours together. Ok! That would give me from Canada all the way down to Patagonia. The whole American continent was mine. But I was afraid of the distance. I had experience with hiring and working with people from coast to coast in one of the widest countries in the world, and I still made it work! So, I knew how to manage remote developers within three or four hours of time difference. That was kind of like my idea. I decided to try where I was from, Guatemala, and Central America in general. When I put up the ad, nobody replied. Remember, this is 2005, right? Nobody replied from Guatemala, from Costa Rica, or anywhere. It had been a week and a half, and I was under a lot of pressure. When all of a sudden, I get an application from someone in Argentina. I thought, *what?! Argentina is like nine thousand kilometers away from here!* But I did the job interview. I was panicking by now because I didn't have anybody to help me with this project and I needed to get it renewed. I told the guy; "This ad isn't for Argentina. Why are you applying?" He said, "What difference does it make? We have exactly the same time zone, so we can work at the same time." I said, "You know what, you're completely right." And I gave him a chance. He started helping me with this prototype and at the end of the month, we did so much work that the client decided to renew the contract for another five months. I was in heaven!

What came after was a lot of hard work. We were able to accomplish it together. We did whatever it took. Once you start your own business, you don't have an eight-hour job anymore. You have to do whatever it takes in order to completely delight your clients so that they will give you more opportunities.

The software wasn't easy. It was an embedded system and we had to make it work with the backend enterprise application. We kept making progress and so our clients stayed happy. At this point, it was only him and I. This guy is still in the company working with me. He's one of our senior architects adding massive value to all our clients and that's exactly how ISU Corp got started (www.isucorp.ca). It's funny because when the contract ended, it was tough but so fulfilling. We were working fourteen hours a day minimum. But because I already had the experience of working full-time for an employer and I also had my part-time gigs; I was already used to working long hours. The difference in this was that the hours were a lot more stressful because we were doing embedded software in a brand-new hardware that didn't exist. We finished the entire deployment exactly within the extra five months they gave us, and I felt so accomplished. I remember when my client said, "David, you guys did an amazing job. Congratulations, this is incredible." And that was that. We started shipping and selling the software. By now, it was July the following year. I was so happy. I never spent a dime from all the contract money that they paid me because I was in saving mode. Remember I started the bank account with $300? I kept adding to it. I completely depended on my wife. I was only taking little bits of money for food and gas, and then the mortgage and all the heavy lifting was done by my wife. Then, when I checked the bank account, I couldn't believe it. In seven months, I had more money saved than I would have gotten full-time in my job in a whole year. But it was because I was very frugal. Those earnings included paying my developer.

During this gig, I met another contractor that had a relationship with different software company that was doing what I wanted to do – the only difference was that these guys were in business for longer and they were considerably bigger. We just started chatting about the possibility of a new project, but nothing really came from it. I tried to find another contract in July. The only problem was that I was unaware that the summer is very bad for selling software contracts. Business gets really slow.

Everybody is playing golf, taking vacations, and I was pounding on doors and ringing up phones. I was getting rejected left, right and centre. People kept telling me to come back in September because they had nothing for me at the time. I was getting blocked and I started to get worried because I wasn't making any money. I started using the savings from the company to foot the bills.

Another interesting thing happened. In the beginnings of the company, I operated from my basement, but because I was now going to the client, it wasn't a very big deal. Once I actually started working from my basement because I was looking for another client, there was a lot of friction that started to occur at home. Number 1: I was a corporate guy. I wanted to feel like I was going to a separate place to do my work. Number 2: When I was at home, my wife thought I was going to be at home with her because that's how it was for the last 15 years. When I came home, I was fully present with my wife and kids. But now that I had my own business, I was at home, but I didn't have time to talk to them because I was working. That came with a lot of conflict, so I decided to go rent a small office. But remember, I was completely frugal. My brother had been in business for a while now. I asked him where I could get a small office where I don't have to pay a lot of rent. He told me about a small apartment that was for rent above one of his stores. He put me in contact with the landlord to see if I could use it. I went in and that was my first office! We didn't have enough money – well, we had the money, but I didn't want to spend it on office furniture, as there was no more money coming in. We instead brought in an old door and two garbage containers, and that was my desk. I didn't spend too much time there anyway since I was always visiting the clients. The rent was so little that it didn't make too big of a dent in the savings. During that summer, since I didn't have any clients, it allowed to me start getting organized.

My brother happened to have a bookkeeper, but he didn't have a lot of work for her. I began needing someone to help with the invoices and other fun things. And he introduced me to Marlene. She is now my office manager, and she's been with me for fifteen years! She's the centre of the company. She's one of the most important people that work with us. I trust her with my life. And she started with five hours a week. Isn't that crazy?

I wasn't making any money, but I was confident I would get another contract. By now, my developer was working with me, so I had to generate income fast to pay him. I started to get stressed out. Fears have a way of overcoming your logic. I was venting to my wife about it and she said, "It's the summer, David. Everybody is on vacation. People are not spending money right now. Why don't you go back home? Take the kids so we don't pay for summer camp and show them our country. Live with your sister for a month and relax. Then come back and find another contract." It made sense to me! I took my two younger kids to Guatemala, lived with my sister, and we made it a very inexpensive trip. I put my kids in school there, which they hated me for! But they learned Spanish, which was fantastic. Now they're happy I made them go that month because they're fluent in Spanish, which is an important skill to foster.

After the month passed, we came back in late August. I thought it was going to be much easier, but it was still hard. I spent three more weeks trying to find a contract and nothing came, until finally, I was able to get a local insurance company to give me a chance to help them with their group benefits applications. As soon as we got in, we signed a six-month contract. I went fully into this business. The other company I had worked for was a mid-sized business. This company was a huge corporation. At the beginning of the contract I was so happy. I was still super humble thanks to the first lesson I learned before. I was grateful for getting this opportunity since I didn't make money over the summer. The contract started to grow, but I was in a cubicle and I felt like I was working for a big corporation yet again. Even though it was my own company, I felt as if I was an employee. But the good thing is that I knew how to work my way around corporate politics. There was a fair share of politics and backstabbing around my project, but I was able to overcome it because I had a lot of years of experience in the corporate world already. By being humble and by being positive, I was able to grow the contract to the point that now, instead of only having two guys, I had four guys. I was making more money. The only problem was that my reputation kept growing, which was wonderful, but I always felt like I wasn't really doing the business myself because I wasn't the one finding the contracts. I was always going to a third party to get my software development gigs. I almost felt like I needed to be able to sell them on my own. Why do I have to rely on somebody else? Obviously at first, it was because I had no reputation and a brand-new business.

All I had was my employment history which was pretty good, and the two little clients that I had during the nights, but they were too little. It was okay, but I started to figure it out. *How do I start selling my own software contracts?*

I started to learn about networking. I bought books on how to network, how to sell, and I realized that selling wasn't for me. That was my **limiting belief.** My limiting belief was this: *I am an excellent architect, a good leader, but I don't want to sell.* I always looked down on sales jobs, which was a mistake. The fact in life is that **everybody is a salesperson**. People just don't know it. They sell their time for money. That makes everybody a salesperson. Everyone has to add value to somebody else in order to survive and thrive in this world. Back then, I thought a salesperson was somebody that cheated and deceived others to get what they wanted. I was completely wrong! I was totally skewed down by my computer science background.

I was able to sell one more contract on the side. I had a big one and a smaller one. I still had my contract with Kim. The company began to grow, and at one point, we were seven guys. I was the manager to one of those guys at the last job I was working at. He wanted to make a move, and because he had been working for the same company all this time, I told him, "If you're willing to risk it, I can give you a job." I gave him a job and he was beside me all the time. We would work on different contracts together. We landed a beautiful contract for one of the largest real estate accounting software companies in North America. This was one of the first wins that I had. I was so happy.

I went back to my mentor, Eric from Bell, asking him how he got his contracts. He said, "David, you have to go to every networking event, and every conference you can." This didn't make any sense to me. How could I do all that if I'm working full time in coding? He told me, "That's why you have to start thinking about delegating your coding and architectural work to somebody else." I didn't want to do it because in my unenlightened mind, I thought I was the best developer in the world, and I didn't want to delegate that part of the entire coding to my team. I was still doing the architecture work and heavy lifting on code reviews. I was still writing the most important pieces of the projects' code. All of this eliminated the chance for me to go and find a contract. If I wanted contracts, I had to go and network and sell and I needed time for that. I didn't have any time. By the way, I was being paid big bucks for being the main architect and developer. The people hiring me were hiring a computer scientist with a lot of reputation. I felt I had to be the one to put in most of the work.

Thanks to this big contract that I was able to land by myself, I had a little more flexibility. When it was time to renew the contract for this big insurance company, because of the environment, I didn't really like it. Back then, I was an expert in Java and in .Net. This company had half the system in Java and half in .Net, so, my company added a lot of value because we were able to build all the good benefits applications from the administrator side on Java and the end-user side where they selected the benefits in .Net. So, they wanted to retain my services, but remember, I was the one facing everybody. I was the one doing the majority of the code. I realized, *you know what, now that I have another mid-sized contract, I'm going to choose not to renew this contract.* I was there for about a year and they wanted me to renew for another year and I said no. I knew they were set to go, and we kept a good relationship with them after that. They would later call us back when I was finally able to sell my business and not just myself. What I was doing at this time was selling myself. People wanted to see me when I actually got the contract. Even the mid-sized company, the owner wanted to see my ass there every day, even though I could do the programming from my own office. In fact, the other guy that I hired – his name is JT, who is one of my best friends now – JT had to be there every single day too, because we had to manage the perception. We had to show up even though a lot of the code was being built by guys in Argentina and Costa Rica. Again, I was still focusing 80% of my time on architecture and development and client relationships. But I didn't know what I didn't know. I did know that I had to get better at selling, and that I needed a mentor.

I thought that I had a real company. We had a contract that was sold by me, but I was having trouble finding another contract. I already had about six or seven people depending on me. We had five guys full-time. The other guys were part-time that I could call at any time and they would dedicate their time for the duration of the project.

From my first project, there was a guy that started working for this software company out of a town close by that had connections in Atlanta and Toronto. They told me that they were hiring developers because they sold a few multi-million-dollar projects. In order to work with them, you had to go through a few interviews. The first interview I had was with a Senior Architect that also ran the business. He liked me, and I liked him, so they sent me to another guy in Toronto who was a Co-Founder. I went to see him, and he was an amazing person. It was the first time I did a contract interview. I was all dressed up. He took me from his house to a pub! He got me drunk beyond belief! It was a strategy, because he wanted to see how I was when I was drinking.

I didn't see an office or anything. It was like I went out for drinks with this guy that I didn't know. Can you imagine? I passed the test. His name was Mark. He asked me if I was ready for my last interview. When I went to the third interview, it was with another guy that flew in from Atlanta to see me. Again, no offices or anything. He took me to a steak house, and we talked for six hours. What he said was, "David, we're about to start a new software product company. I'm taking the best guys from this current company and I want to shut down the software consulting business because I'm losing money. I know how to sell, but I don't know how to deliver." And then I told him, "I know how to deliver, but I don't know how to sell!" I thought I was going to get a small software contract with this guy, but instead, he said, "You know what, if you're willing to become the acting CEO of this company, I can teach you how to sell, and then you can teach me how to deliver. We can work out an arrangement where your company is subcontracted to me and whatever we work on, you can also bring your people." I was in heaven! What an opportunity. We shook hands, he took me down to Atlanta, and we did some team building. Now, the tough part came. I was now running two companies. I was running my company and his company from the operation side. This includes accounting, administration, and everything. At this point, I was still coding. My mentor said "David, what are you doing? Now you have this guy, the contract with the real estate company, the software contract with these guys, and a contract with people who they themselves have three big contracts." He was right. All of a sudden, I had twenty developers that were reporting to me, and they were losing money. I had to investigate why they were losing money and why they couldn't deliver. When I looked into it, the coding guys had a lot of freedom, but there wasn't enough discipline in order to be able to deliver on time and under budget. Unfortunately, because the company had no money, I had to let a lot of the coders go. I only kept one project manager and everybody else had to go. I took them from losing a million dollars a year to making $800,000. We were super happy. My new partner – we considered each other partners even though we hadn't signed anything official – started teaching me how to network, start meeting people, and how to close deals. I started teaching him how to deliver. Today, he's one of my best friends. This guy that was put in charge of operations, his name is Tommy, he was my side kick. We had an amazing run. We were both learning so much from each other and both companies started to grow. We eventually were selling and delivering together. I managed the technical end of the sales process and he would open the doors.

The relationship lasted for a while. During this, one of my mentors told me "David, if you don't delegate 100% and uninstall your compilers, I will never give you a word of advice again. What you're doing is stupid. You're still doing your architecture work and development when you have other guys. You have bigger responsibilities. Stop wasting your time. You're better than that." I finally paid attention and did it. I was so afraid to remove the compilers from my computer and start dedicating myself 100% to leadership. But it was the best decision I ever made in my life.

**If you're not growing, you're dying.** It's impossible to stay in the same spot. Either you're growing or you're moving backwards and shrinking. If you have mentors and you don't pay attention to what they're telling you, it's useless to have them. You have to conquer your fears and realize that everything is going to be okay.

I finally removed my compilers and took up my role as the CEO of my own company and as the acting CEO of this other software company. Everything started to prosper. Imagine if I didn't remove my compilers! I could have never moved past a certain amount of sales because I was the main one doing the software. The lesson was profound. As soon as I followed my mentor's advice, everything started to prosper. Now I had the time to be a proper leader and learn how to sell. I could also teach how to deliver.

Everything was going well, and we stayed together like this for a couple of years. A lot of my business was at this point 50% through this other company and 50% through mine, ISU Corp (www.isucorp.ca). I never had the necessity to grow my local team. I still had a team of five people. I was more focused on learning how to sell through my partnership. I also had the responsibility to teach them how to deliver, too. That was the deal. We stopped the bleeding. My business was okay, it wasn't exploding, but it was doing well! I never had the scarcity mentality anymore because work was coming in steadily. The real estate contract was going really well, and it was growing. We proved to them that we could actually do it. That required a lot of work and I used the subcontractor model. I was very careful about hiring full-time people because I knew I was project-based. I started hiring sub-contractors and making sure I was using temporary people so that when a project ended, I wouldn't go bankrupt.

As the relationship with my partner grew, we started to attract bigger and better clients. All of a sudden, we landed a huge client that could make us or break us.

It would also make or break me.

## Golden Nuggets:

- **If you're not growing, you're dying.** It's impossible to stay in the same spot. Either you're growing or you're moving backwards and shrinking. If you have mentors and you don't pay attention to what they're telling you, it's useless to have them. You have to conquer your fears and realize that everything is going to be okay.
- If you want to be an exceptional business owner, you must learn how to delegate and inspire your team to be the best they can become.

# 9

# Here We Grow

*From 9 coders to over 120 in less than 12 months.*

"Everyone wants to live on top of the mountain,
but all the happiness and growth occurs while
you are climbing it."
— Andy Rooney

Let's just rewind for a minute. Remember how I had that office on the second floor of my brother's store? From there, as soon as I got some more money through contracts, my brother rented me one of his properties to use as an office. I moved there with Marlene and the developers that were with me at the time. I was renting a basement; it was three times the size, but it was a basement, nonetheless. I had this idea that in order for me to attract better clients, I had to have a better reputation. I thought, *Okay. How do you get a better reputation? It must be to have an office in a prestigious building.* I started researching what that would be like. I looked into where law firms, banks, government buildings, and other important organizations had their offices. I checked out a few buildings and wondered if they had anything up for rent. When I saw the cost of them, I knew I couldn't pay anything. But sometimes, life plays out in wonderful ways.

My mentor, Eric, as you'll recall, was really good at playing squash. He also happened to live in the same town as me. When I stopped working for Bell and started working in Toronto, and even later on when I started my own business, Eric would ask me to come out and play some squash. The racket club we played at had a newsletter they'd print once a month. I was reading the newsletter in the cafeteria one day when I saw that they had a little closet that they were willing to rent out in a nice office building.

The coincidence was that the owner of the racket club was the owner of one of the most prestigious high-rise buildings in town. I went up and asked about this place he had for rent. It was very small, about 900sq ft. The owner of the building came and talked to me – his name was Brad Marsland. I was so impressed. This guy owned several buildings in town, and he was a multi-millionaire! I got a bit intimidated. I asked him how much it would be to rent out this small space. When I showed him the ad, he explained, "Oh! That Ad isn't very useful anymore. We're using that space as storage now, but I could show it to you anyway if you'd like." He opens this thing up and it's basically a closet. It's full of desks, chairs and garbage. I asked him how much it was... and I still couldn't afford it! I really couldn't, even though it was the smallest space in the whole building. The beautiful part though was that it was right beside Brad's own office, which was the penthouse. It was at the very top floor which felt very prestigious. Naturally, I really wanted this, so I told him I'd figure it out. I asked him if we could do a one-year lease, and he said no. Minimum was five years. It was a huge risk. I was a project-based business, so I had no guarantee that I was going to keep making money.

Sometimes, I'd go for breakfast to meet other people that were in the same industry as I was. Through one of these events, I met someone named Jason. I started with .Net, and Jason told me he wanted to start his business using PHP and Open Source. We had breakfast one day and we hit it off. I asked him if he had an office. He said no – he couldn't afford an office. He said he was working out of his apartment and it was driving him crazy. I said, "You know, I found a small space. I bet we could fit two desks in it. If you wanna go 50/50, we can rent it out together. But it's a five-year commitment." We went to see the space together this time. Brad Marsland thought it was funny that someone was really interested in renting it out, because this was literally his closet. I made the contract under my name and subcontracted Jason to help with the other half because Brad didn't want two contracts. And we moved in! Brad cleaned it up, removed all the junk, painted and laid down carpet. It was a beautiful tiny office with the view of the city, on the top floor. I was so happy.

Ok, now remember the real estate contract? A big part of why we landed that contract was because the owner investigated us and saw that I had an office at the Marsland centre. That's right – although it's a surface level difference, the reputation of having an office created new opportunities for me.

This is an example of why I consider myself to be a life hacker. Building your own business is one of the most difficult things a person can do in his or her life. That's why it is imperative that you find all these details that are relatively simple to cover that will go a long way down the road. Not everything has to be difficult when you learn how to life hack. This is one of the reasons why I'm writing this book. We're in the middle of the book now, and I'm hoping that my stories are going to influence you into making the jump. It's worth trying it out on your own, and life hacking will help you make it. Because eventually, you're going to make it! If you're resourceful enough, if you grow to have nerves of steel, and you're an honest person, you will eventually make it. Once you do, it feels amazing. It feels like you've conquered the world. This office was one of the things I used to start getting more contracts, and it actually worked out. The office played a big part in my psychology as well. You have to find something that pushes your mental state into a state of abundance. **You need to already feel successful to attract more wealth into your life**, and that is what this office meant for me.

When I worked at my last job, I was blessed enough to buy my dream car. It was a BMW convertible, 325 injected. One year before I married my wife, I told her, "One day, I'm going to have a BMW convertible". Ever since then, that was in the back of my mind. The last year that I was on the job, I was able to find the car and I finally owned it. If you've ever had the opportunity to drive the car of your dreams, then you know the feeling I got when I rode off in the vehicle I wanted for all those years. It made me feel so successful. I kept it for twenty years.

It accomplished the same thing as the office did – I felt legitimate, and that made potential clients see me the same way. At that time in my life, it made me feel successful which gave me the confidence to go and get more contracts and attract more wealth into my life. **It's not about being defined by material possessions – it's about surrounding yourself with the things that will push your psychology into high gear to achieve your full potential.**

This is another thing that you must know: **reputation is the only thing you have in business**. Reputation and your work to back it up. I'm only as good as my last successful client. One of the mottos in my company is that we're willing to bleed out of business in order to delight a client. The only reason why we're in business is to add massive value to our clients. We think of our clients first and foremost. We think of their well-being, and then we have the right to think about our own well-being. In the beginning, you don't filter out clients because you want to take all the work you can get. As a result of that, I had a couple of clients that took advantage of it, and we ended up working for free for a long time until they were happy. But they were taking advantage of us. I remember the worst-case scenario had happened when I worked six whole months for free and I ended up about $500,000 in the hole, and we almost went bankrupt. When we finally made the client happy, we made them realize what they were doing to us. We still got a reference out of that client. That's the attitude you need to not only survive, but to thrive. You don't have to be good – you have to be better than good. Not excellent, but better than excellent. You have to be outstanding. You have to be exceptional. Or you die.

So, back to what this chapter is about!

As we started growing both businesses in Atlanta and Toronto, we got bigger clients. I remember one day I was at my house, and we were walking the dog when I got a call from my business partner. He said, "David, I have a big opportunity. It's a huge risk. This could be a 10 to 20-million-dollar contract, but you have to be willing to do this." By then, I was working out of my office and I was going to see clients. Our clients were all over the place. We had people in Vancouver and in Atlanta, and it was a nice work environment. I still only had five full-time employees. All together we only had twelve developers. We had worked it out beautifully, but we were still playing in the small league. By now, my business partner had a start-up with another founder, so he was beginning to really focus on that. But, this opportunity landed in his lap. It was through one of his mentors! **Your mentors will not only teach you how to live your life better without making the same mistakes they made, but they will also give you the connections you need in order to achieve breakthroughs.** I remember asking my wife if we were ready for the big leagues. This had the potential to become a huge deal.

The client was in Toronto, and the project was to do a videogame online. By now I had done ERP software from the ground up, accounting, real estate and lots of insurance systems, and everything around finance – you name it. We even did a software product for the University of Waterloo that aided ethical research for the human and animal research department.

However, we hadn't done anything to do with gaming before. For me, gaming was foreign. The last time I remembered playing a game was when a Doom-like game came around in '96. I had a network with seven computers, and I made the game run in the network. I couldn't believe I could actually see my character in the game. From there, I hadn't done anything else with that. I was always about productivity, and video games never really caught my attention.

We went to sell this contract. Normally, the life of a game software development project is about two to three years. That's the standard amount of time a team needs to make a game, but these guys were in trouble. They were one year into the game and they barely had 10% of the game done. It was because they wanted to disrupt the industry. They wanted to make a 3D game that would run on a web browser, which at that point, had never been done before. Usually, those 3D games were on DVD's because it required a lot of graphics and bandwidth to run them. They wanted to create a break-through. As a result, they were losing a lot of money, the morale was low, they already had more than a hundred developers on this game, full-time. But nothing worked! This is why they hired us. We were completely honest. I told them, "I have never written a game in my life, but I know how to run a software company, I know how to hire the best people, and I can promise you that if you give us the chance, we will do whatever it takes to fix this." This must sound familiar to you by now, right? Learn the lingo!

We started with all the people that we could find in Canada. I grabbed seven guys and we said, *here we go!* We did a run trial for a couple of months and we actually managed to fix a lot of their issues. I realized there was a big problem between the artists, designers, front end, back end, and peer developers. We're talking about a hundred-person job, and there was a huge cultural problem. It's not a small project with three people on it. We proved that we could deliver on time, and they gave us the entire project. We agreed to run it with the core of our business, the best of the best. The next step was to grow the team because we needed more hands to tackle the project alongside us.

A couple of problems came up. I was already used to working from my office, which felt like freedom. Now I had to go see this client based in an area far past Toronto every day. I was commuting again, and not only that – it was officially the longest commute I ever had to do. One of the reasons I opened my own business was so that I didn't have to drive to Toronto anymore, but this opportunity was crazy, and I didn't want to let it go. It meant I had to be there every day because of the scale of the project, and I was in the center fixing the cultural and technological issues. At the same time, I had to start doing lots of travelling because I had to grow exponentially. I started putting ads all over the place trying to get the best developers that I could, locally and remotely. Wherever I could find the rock stars, I would go. But I completely forgot about finding people with the same values as I had. My values were also changing. The project lasted for a while. We were in the first year when something started to shift in me.

Remember my gratefulness? My attitude of "Thank you for today"? That started to wear out because now, we were millions and millions of dollars into a project and I started to grow both companies exponentially. Actually, it almost looked like one company by now, but it was all through subcontracting invoices. We were never legally bound even though I had all the responsibility of the other company. Little by little, greed started to find its way inside me again. I started to feel more important. As I was depositing checks for millions of dollars in the bank account, I started to feel that I was responsible for this, and my greed started to show. Again, the same way – the little monster I could have killed many times, I allowed to grow. It grew until I felt I was the best entrepreneur in the world, and I deserved everything. That started to create big problems with my partners.

The environment was high stress as well. By the way, a game project is one of the most difficult things a software development company can do. I've even done rocket science projects. I was in charge of building all the software infrastructure for a company that manages all the vessels in the world through eight satellites. I have literally done rocket science projects successfully. And this project was ten times harder. Gaming projects are harder because the people that have to work on the projects come from very different backgrounds. They're artists mixed with computer scientists and businesspeople, and none of them talk to each other properly. Managing those relationships will wear you down really fast.

My first employee and one of the best coders I know is from Argentina. I thought, *you know what, let's hire more people from there.* The majority of our hiring became Argentina and Canada. However, in Argentina, we needed to house all these people, so I was in charge of finding two floors in a high-rise building in downtown Buenos Aires. I was travelling to Argentina every three weeks, and I loved it. At the beginning, I loved the culture, the environment, and I became best friends with Diego who was a developer in the project that I'm still great friends with today. He helped me with the hiring process.

We had so many problems building a company in Argentina with all the legal entities and all the bureaucracy. I had to do personal guarantees in the office, and it was a five-year lease. It was crazy. We rented two floors from a brand new twenty story building. I learned so much from this process. I kept learning. The first year was fantastic because I was still humble. When I told you about the little monster, this happened in the second year of this big project. The monster got bigger.

Alongside the monster, I had another problem. I started to neglect my wife. The weeks that I was in Canada, I was going to Toronto and coming back at midnight. I was in Toronto so much that I had a room set aside for me at the local hotel that was a few blocks from the client because sometimes I had to stay over. The last meeting was at midnight and we'd have to be back early the next morning. Though, I was so blessed to have my VP of Operations taking care of my other clients. I was 100% focused on this one client. I finally learned how to delegate, I guess. By then, I hadn't written a line of code in two years. I was growing exponentially, and it was all really exciting. Money was flowing through. It felt like we had made it. The more I acquired developers, the more I felt like I was responsible for them, but I also felt more empowered. I had more confidence and that was helping with the project. We'd actually found a gaming engine that would run online with 3D, but we still had to figure out the graphics, file sizes, music, and everything. It was growing, and the project was working. The client was happy. We were selling millions and millions of dollars. But my CFO was always warning me.

"David, one client is 90% of your work with both companies combined." **This one single client was responsible for 90% of our revenue, and that's one of the most dangerous mistakes you can make in a business,** but I didn't know. My CFO, John, was telling me every single quarter, "You need to sell another big project, otherwise this could bite us in the ass." You know what I said? "I don't care, let's milk this cow and see how much we can grow this client." We grew from one guy to over 120 guys in one year.

However, like I said, by the end of the first year, I started to get greedy. Why? Because I was tired. I was tired of the travelling. Tired of all the risk. I was tired of the relationship because I felt like my partner's company was my company – only, it wasn't. I was a subcontractor to him all this time. I started to get things all wrong. I felt like I was putting in more effort in the game than he was. That started to make me proud, arrogant, and it transformed me into a bad person. The amount of stress that I had combined with all the travelling, bureaucracy, and all the problems that come with managing so many people with so little time – it was really hurting me. I started expressing it all with greed and a bad attitude. I started neglecting my family. I started fighting a lot with my wife, and my kids didn't know who I was anymore because I was never home. It all started to wear down on me. The world was caving in.

With so many problems came many lessons. One of the greatest lessons comes with the next part of my story.

## Golden Nuggets

- Never have a single client be accountable for more than 30% of your net revenue. If you do, the client ends, and your company goes out of business. A healthy amount is 25-30% max. You can have a large client, but don't let it be more than 30% of your revenue. If you do, you have to do whatever it takes to get another client to level it out. You have to have the risk divided into three or four different clients.
- If you're resourceful enough, if you grow to have nerves of steel, and you're an honest person, **you will eventually make it.**
- **You need to already feel successful to attract more wealth into your life.**
- Reputation is **everything**.
- Your mentors will not only teach you how to live your life better without making the same mistakes they made, but they will also give you the connections you need in order to achieve **breakthroughs.**

# 10

# Nervous Breakdown

*How much can we take?*

"Sometimes, breaking down is the bravest thing you can do."
– Vironika Tugaleva

I worked so hard on this project that I was beginning to feel that my partner's company was my company. I was the Managing Director, and I was a partner. But the true fact was that the majority owner was him. I was beginning to develop resentment. The extreme stress began to affect my personal life, my business life, and on top of that, the commute to Toronto was getting pretty bad. My resentment started to grow. Once you have resentment in your heart, you change appreciation for expectation. That is one of the worst mistakes you could ever make. Ego is built upon fear. When you're expecting, it's because you fear you won't get what you want. Pay close attention to this because it was probably one of the biggest mistakes I've ever made. It almost cost me my life.

I was driving back and forth from Toronto one of those winter days. The day before, it had taken me three hours to get home. I was completely exhausted. I had to be at the office for 8 am. I didn't see my family for such a long time that I decided to drive back to them. I got home around midnight, just to wake up at four in the morning the next day. Something that began to happen around this time was that I was trying to unconsciously balance myself out using alcohol. Everything started with a small glass of wine because they say one or two cups a day is beneficial for your health. Bullshit! The problem is that, sure, having one cup of wine a day is good for your health, but it can also be a catalyst for you to become an alcoholic. It relaxes you, and when it relaxes you when you're in a high-stress environment, you're going to want more whether you realize it or not.

I was in such a messed-up place at this time of my life. The last workout I had done was years ago. My entire life was dedicated to making this project successful. The only escape route that my body had was the alcohol. By the end of this journey, I was drinking a whole bottle of wine by myself every single day. I was risking becoming an alcoholic, because I was using it as medicine to bring down my stress.

So, the day I went back home only to commute back to Toronto was in the middle of February. A huge ice storm hit followed by a fierce snowstorm. This all affected the highway. When I hit halfway through my drive, I was already four hours in. My heart started palpitating. Every time I saw another accident, it began palpitating with more urgency. I saw three accidents, and one of them was definitely lethal because I saw emergency helicopters airlifting people away. I thought to myself, *Oh my god. That could be me. That could have been me. I've been sitting in traffic for four hours. I'm only halfway through, and for what? For what? I'm not getting anything!* At the end of the day, I wasn't even a majority shareholder in this whole thing. It was only my ego feeding my ego. It was me trying to demonstrate to the world that I could do it. And I actually did it. For two years, the project was completely successful. But it was killing me.

Once I reached the last accident, I felt a terrible pain in my left arm that went all the way up to my chest. I got really scared. I got off the highway and stopped at a town that was by the main road. I tried to calm myself down. I remember it so clearly. By now, it was noon and I knew I couldn't do this to myself anymore. The chest pain started to go away little by little, but I got really scared. I turned back, and I drove home. I called in sick and I went right to the doctor.

When I saw her, she told me I hadn't been there for five years. I knew I had been neglecting my health in order to grow my business. I realized that something was wrong. I told her about the pain in my chest and how afraid I was. I didn't know what was going on. The doctor looked grave. She sent me straight to the hospital to get tests done. They put electrodes on my chest to test my heart. They administered a stress test where I had to run on a treadmill. One week later, the results came back. The doctor called me urgently to her office. She said, "David, you had a pre-heart attack. It's called an angina. It was so strong that it almost became a full heart attack. Two percent stronger, and you could have died. Look at yourself. You're in a complete mess. The environment that you have put yourself in is deteriorating your health." She then asked me if I was drinking alcohol. I said yes. I told her I was drinking a bottle of wine a day. She said I was using it as medicine, and that the alcohol was keeping me alive because it was the only thing that was calming down my nerves. But it was also fucking up my system! It calmed my anxiety and made me more productive because I could push more, but it was fucking up the rest of my body. She said that there were only two alternatives. "I can give you these pills. They will help you manage your stress and will lower your anxiety, but you will get addicted within one to two months. Or, you can change your lifestyle. You are a forty-year-old man, you have a future ahead of you still. You're hardworking and smart, but you're killing yourself with work and this is no way to live, David." For this brief moment, my doctor became my counsellor. She saw the pain that I was in and I really didn't have anyone else in my life that I could talk to about personal things. I had cut everybody out of my life to be completely focused on growing the business. She said, "Whatever it is you're going through, you have to make a radical change. I'll give you the pills anyway because I know it's going to take you time to decide on what you're going to do. But the warning is, if you take this pill for more than thirty days, you will have a high risk of becoming addicted. I want you to stop the alcohol right away, take these pills instead, and change your lifestyle. You have to reconnect with your family, and you have to re-evaluate your life." After this conversation, it felt like I experienced a breakthrough.

A breakthrough happens for two reasons: when you have enough pain or when you have enough pleasure. That's when you decide to change dramatically. In this case, my breakthrough was because I had enough pain to push me into change. I realized I had to change my life completely. That day I went back home, I apologized to my wife and kids, and I told them that I needed to make up for all the time I had lost. I told them I was going to break the relationship I had with my partner.

The next day, I had a phone call with him and told him I was going to fly to Atlanta to talk about our future. I got onto the plane, and it wasn't a moment of fear. I felt humble and happy. I was grateful because my sister in-law lived in Atlanta. I stayed with her instead of staying in a hotel and she saw how fucked up I was that she gave me a couple of pills just to be able to relax and sleep. I don't even know what she gave me, but it allowed me to calm my nerves and go break up with my partner, who was also my best friend.

The next day, we set up a breakfast meeting. I sat down with him and he knew. He completely knew that I was going to end it because I couldn't stop shaking. My eyes were red and watering, and I told him that I was in over my head. It was 100% my fault. I took full responsibility. I told him, "I got greedy. I got proud. I developed a huge ego based on the success of this project. At the same time, I neglected my health, my spirituality, and my family. It's time for something to change. I almost had a heart attack. My doctor told me to change my lifestyle, and I know that if I continue with you, I'm going to end up either in the hospital, in a wheelchair, dead, or lonely without my wife and kids. That's way more valuable to me than any amount of money in the world. You need somebody else to run this." I told him he could keep all the clients I made with him, and I would keep my old clients (which didn't even pay for half the payroll at this point), and I wished him the best. He understood. I apologized first, and then he apologized as well. We hugged, cried, and that was the beginning of a beautiful relationship with him outside of business.

I came back home, and it took about two months for me to sign all the legal papers and to redeem all the assets back to him. I was the managing partner, so I was the legal representative of his company in Canada and Argentina. I fixed all that mess with the revenue agency and the government. While I was doing that, I told my wife, "Honey, we have to get out of here. I want to go to Thailand. Get a one-way ticket for you and the kids and do whatever you need to do to get them out of school. If they have to do the year over, it's okay. Let them. I'd rather they repeat a grade than lose them. Please, go talk to the principals because I don't know when we're coming back. Let's go as soon as possible."

My wife got tickets for the first week of May, and I was so excited. I was in such a bad state that for the first time in my life, I didn't care about the payroll or how much money I had in the bank. I didn't care about anything. I just picked up the phone and talked to my VP of Operations, and I told him "Felix, listen, brother. I need to go away and fix myself. I don't know if we're going to have a business when I get back. I know the few clients we have left is not going to make ends meet. I know we're not going to meet all of our expenses. If I come back and there's no business, you're a brilliant guy, I'm a brilliant guy, everyone in the company has a good head on their shoulders, and I'm confident we can all go find jobs." Felix told me, "Don't worry about anything. God is in control. Go fix yourself and reconnect with your family. I'm sure we'll still be here when you get back, whenever you decide to return."

I took a plane to Thailand with my family. On purpose, I never turned on my laptop or my phone. I brought them with me because it would give me more anxiety not to have them around, but I never turned them on. We started a beautiful experience on this trip with my wife and my two younger kids. We got to Thailand, we went to Khao San Road, we were backpacking all over because we were on a freaking tight budget. But, the backpacking experience was amazing. We stayed at this beautiful hotel called the Buddy Lodge which is in the party area of Bangkok, and the four of us had an amazing time. By then, my kids were in grade 11 and grade 8. We took them out of school two months before the end of the year and we didn't care about them failing any classes. Of course, they didn't after all. I just knew that I needed to reconnect with them and that this was the starting point of my new life.

Two weeks into the trip, we were moving from town to town until we hit an island called Kho Phi Phi, which is south of Thailand. It was a beautiful place. This island doesn't have cars or motorcycles. Everyone walks or uses a bicycle. It's gorgeous. It had white sandy beaches and amazingly kind people. It's full of backpackers. Once I got there, I remembered that my doctor told me to get into an activity that would help me relax. I already had one certification I did for scuba diving a few years back, but even that which I knew I loved I had forgotten about in all the mess. When I was on the island, I thought, *you know what? I'm gonna get the advanced open water certification.* So, the next day, I found a scuba diving school. It was low season in Thailand, so the owner of the company gave me the best diving instructor he had. He was a beautiful soul from England. I was the only client! I paid for the second certification, but because there were no other customers, he told me he'd teach me things that don't belong in the course. He said, "If you're up for it, we can do four or five dives a day and you'll get a lot more for your money." I said, bring it on! I was waking up at 7am, diving the whole day and coming back at 6pm. Sometimes we would even do a night dive. It was fabulous. Actually, the night dive that we did was my final exam.

I was focused on diving and my family, and I experienced wonderful things under the water. The diving helped me a lot, because when you're diving, your breathing has to be really nice and slow. It's impossible to get stressed if you're breathing that way. By the way, if you get stressed under the ocean, you'd die immediately! It's impossible to get stressed if you want to survive. My diving instructor taught me how to control my breath under water. He would sometimes pull off my mask thirty metres under water and I knew exactly what I had to do. I'd put my emergency mask on, I'd open my eyes, and clear my mask. Sometimes we'd be diving 25 metres under water and he would pull off one of my fins and I was fine. I'd know where he was, I'd go and get it. He made me a master at controlling stress and fear, without any chemicals. In fact, the first day that I got onto the plane, I brought the pills with me, but I never took them again. I didn't feel the need to take them. My heart would race, but I would try to calm myself down. I didn't know anything about meditation back then. But I realized that scuba diving was a form of meditation. I had to be 100% focused on what I was doing and be aware of my surroundings. At the end of the trip, I earned my advanced open-water certification, but I also learned how to do cave diving, how to manage high stress under water while still staying relaxed, and that's the tool that God used to start teaching me that I don't need any medication, drugs or alcohol in order to stay in a peaceful state.

From Thailand, we took a plane to Bali. It was my dream to go to Bali because my older brother goes there often. We got there and stayed in a beautiful villa close to the ocean with a private pool. We had our own cook. He was a nice kid who we later helped out by giving him some funding for his studies. I had an amazing time. Two weeks into Bali, I told my wife, "Okay. I think I'm ready to go back. I feel perfect." By then, I had gone four weeks without any panic attacks or stress. I didn't have any pills or alcohol. The only alcohol I had was for fun, and not for self-medicating, which was completely different.

Two days before going back, I started wondering what was going on with the company. Now that I felt relaxed, I turned on my laptop and holy shit! I had close to a thousand emails! I started laughing because I couldn't believe it. I didn't really care much about the emails, but I just read some of the ones from Felix. He was mostly just wishing that I was doing well. But then I noticed that one of my best buddies from before emailed me.

I hired this guy a while back when I was still in a Senior Development position at one of the last companies I worked for. We needed to do a SharePoint implementation. So, I hired a contractor to get it going. Out of the five companies I chose, this guy was the best because he was the most honest. We became very good friends once the implementation was done. Serendipitously, I found this same guy in another networking event about a year later. Thanks to that, he switched jobs and he was then representing another development company that was under stress, and he got me a contract with a government organization to create business intelligence platform for managing four billion dollars a year. That project ended, and I forgot about it. It had been about four years since then.

When I opened my laptop, I saw about seven emails from him, saying *David, where are you? I need you!* I thought, holy shit! I emailed him back asking how he was doing. I hoped everything was okay. I was worried, and I called him right away. He told me he was the Development Director for this company in town. He said, "We're under a lot of stress. What's happening is crazy. I need to know if you can get us out of trouble. I'm going to connect you with our CEO." Of course, I agreed. I told him I was going back home in three days and that she could talk to me this way for the time being. The next day, I phoned her. Then she gave me the news: "David, as soon as you come home there is a contract waiting for you. Brad has been talking beautiful things about you."

I came back. That contract ended up being a million-dollar project. It saved my business, and it saved my life. Recalling this miracle still makes me feel so grateful. I was able to keep the beautiful people that started the company with me many years before. Those were the only guys that were kept because everybody else was hired for their technical knowledge and not their attitude. I was focused only on the growth of the company and not my personal and spiritual growth. That contract allowed me to get back on my feet and to start rethinking what the meaning of life was and how I should run my business, my relationships, *and my life.* I came back with that project waiting for me. I had to hire a couple more people and we were able to pay back all the debts and taxes. It gave me a second wind. Now, I was completely on my own, with no partner, and no excuses. I was a different man. And then I realized, *Okay. There's something I don't know yet. Something has to change to make this last.*

One of my first buddies who I shared a tiny office with at the Marsland centre gave me a book before he left. He said it was going to change my life. He told me he was applying the book in his day-to-day and that it was completely changing his life. I ignored it at first because I came from a corporate background where the only option was putting in extra time and effort in order to succeed. I didn't immediately trust what sounded like a cheap way to skip out on hard work, but that wasn't what this was at all.

The book was called "The Four-Hour Work Week" by Tim Ferriss. It was the first tool that God used on me to start teaching me about universal laws. It was what I needed to find a balance in my hectic life. Like the law of gravity, there is something called Pareto's Law, or the Pareto Principle. It's known as the 80/20 rule, and it exists everywhere in the world. We don't know why it exists, the same way we don't know exactly why the law of gravity exists, but it's there. We can measure it, and it's consistent. As I started reading this book, I began to realize all the mistakes I had made in the past. It made me see how I was wasting energy and spreading myself thin for things that I could be accomplishing with more efficiency. I thought long and hard on how I could simplify my life.

Wouldn't it be nice to be successful **while also enjoying all that life has to offer?** Isn't that what life is all about?

## Golden Nuggets

- A breakthrough happens for two reasons: when you have enough **pain** or when you have enough **pleasure**.
- Don't let greed destroy what's really important in your life. Be aware of your **attitude** and **outlook**.
- There are ways to use your time and energy more efficiently so that you can achieve all you want to achieve without burning out.
- Never neglect your **health**.
- Never neglect your **family**.
- Never neglect your **spirituality**.

# 11

# Hacking Life 101

"The ability to simplify means to eliminate the unnecessary so that the necessary may speak."

– Martin G. Fischer

Now you know why I had to leave everything behind and reconnect with my family. I was working through some trauma and almost had a heart attack because of all the stress I put myself under. I was working insanely hard for someone else's success, and I found myself in one of the hardest moments of my life. I hit a hard reset and took off to Thailand with my family. But this wasn't a permanent solution. I knew I needed something that would prevent me from going back to my old ways.

Something that helped change my life for the better is the book I mentioned before, "The Four-Hour Work Week". A central teaching in this book is Pareto's law. I believe that it's one of the most important strategies that I've used that has helped me live a life of happiness and fulfillment.

When I started the company in 2005, I did so with the intention of giving myself the freedom to work from home. After working for ten to fifteen years in the corporate world, I realized that a lot of the hours I spent sitting at the office was wasted time, and that I didn't need to be there. I thought, *why do I have to be stuck in a cubicle all day to get paid?* I couldn't employ a lot of the methodologies I wanted to try because people have systems in place. Companies have processes and rules, and more often than not, my way of thinking wasn't compatible with those rules. That was another factor pushing me towards starting my own business.

When I got started, I thought *okay, I'm finally going to work from home.* The first couple of months didn't go so well. Reason number one was that I was accustomed to having my own office. Number two, when my wife saw me at home, she wanted me to be with her and the kids. When I was at home now, I was working and couldn't spend time with them like before. It created a bit of a conflict, and I realized there had to be a divide to keep the peace. I decided I would try working from Starbucks, but that got tiring, too. I didn't want reoccurring expenses until I raked in enough revenue and cash flow into the company. Let's fast forward through the struggle to find an office (in case you already forgot, this story is in chapter 9).

As I mentioned before, I was able to get this nice office with Jason. As my reputation grew, I got more office space as well. All of a sudden, Jason told me, "David, I read this book. Have you ever heard of Pareto's law? I think I'm going to start applying it to my life." Basically, the law says that 80% of the results comes from 20% of the effort, and it happens everywhere. I thought it was crazy and impossible. I came from an environment where the mentality is that you have to put in tons and tons of work and effort to have all the results you want. In reality, 80% of your effort is 20% of your results.

If you can find ways to use this rule to your advantage, you can simplify your life to the max, and achieve enormous results with minimal effort. They have done studies on this. For example, if you look at any city's roads, 80% of the traffic goes on 20% of the roads. They have measured this everywhere. If you look at a company's sales year after year, 80% of the total earnings comes from 20% of the clients – that's nuts.

Jason was the first person in my life to set the example on how to use this law. He decided that he was going to leave the office and that he didn't want to renew the contract anymore. He said, "I'm gonna see if I can work from the next city away from me. I'm not going to be in this office anymore." I wished him well and told him to let me know how it goes. He was hoping he wouldn't lose any clients. He went to the next city over while his clients remained in the city where we were. Nothing happened. His business survived the move. After a year, he said "Okay, I'm gonna try living in the United States." He went to work from Texas, and he was still hoping he wouldn't lose any clients. Sure enough, he didn't! I was paying close attention to what he was doing. Every few months we'd chat and catch up. One time, he said, "I wonder if I can work from France and not lose any clients." I thought he was crazy. He moved to France and he didn't lose any clients. Finally, he made the ultimate decision to move somewhere where the time zone change was very drastic. He said, "I wonder if I can work from New Zealand." He went, with a time zone change of over 12 hours, and he still didn't lose any clients! In fact, he made a couple more clients. Once he was in New Zealand, he became an airplane pilot. He enjoyed the country with his girlfriend, now his wife. What he ended up doing was he got rid of 80% of his clients and only kept the 20% that was giving him most of the revenue. And there you have it. His life was completely simplified. What I also noticed was that his stress level was almost non-existent.

Before Jason told me about The Four-Hour Work Week book, one of my mentors told me that I should read the 80/20 Manager by Richard Koch. It basically explains how to become a better leader and manager by applying Pareto's law. But when I read it, I just got confused. I really couldn't understand how 80% of the results come from only 20% of the effort. Actually, there are extreme cases where its 95/5, when 95% of the results come from 5% of the effort. I read that book and it just didn't work for me. Then I read a book called 80/20 Sales and Marketing by Perry Marshall and the same thing happened. That isn't to say that these books aren't well written – it's just helpful to get the groundwork of 80/20 down before going into more specific applications of the principle. Four-Hour is a great foundation for this.

The way Tim Ferriss writes his books are so simple and down to earth. His books taught me about the "new rich", which is basically living life on your own terms and defining how much money you need to live without comparing yourself to anybody else. That's what my biggest conflict was at this point of my life. I thought I needed to make millions and millions and wear suits and be this high-end guy. I was full of pride, and pride will kill you. It goes hand-in-hand with ego. **You'll never be fulfilled if you're full of pride and run by ego.**

I've read The Four-Hour Work Week four times. Once in a while I'll read it again because the principles are so intense. When Tim Ferriss decided to write this book, what he went through before getting there is impressive, too. Before you read any other material that applies Pareto's law, start with The Four-Hour Work Week, then you'll understand all the other books – which by the way, I read them again and finally understood thanks to The Four-Hour Work Week.

When Jason was going through this experiment, I was going through all the problems that I have already mentioned to you in this book. I was doing the complete opposite of what he was doing. I was trying to grow as fast as I could with as many employees as I could. I was only focused on the growth of the company and not even the net profits, but the gross sales, which makes no sense.

Let me give you a quick example, because this is important for when you have your own business. If I sell 10 million dollars and I lose $500,000, it's less than if I sell 1 million dollars and I make $100,000 profit. To sell a million dollars and make $100,000 profit is a lot easier than the first scenario. This is what you have to really analyze. People think that sales are everything, but it's nothing without the net profits. You have to look at the bottom line and you have to look at your cash flow.

After all this, and after I went through my crisis, Jason's example was the reason why I decided to just take off and risk it for thirty days. I actually went with the idea that, because I was spiritually, mentally and physically broken inside, I didn't care if I lost my business. I had enough pain to take the risk and try what Jason did. I went to southeast Asia for thirty days. I already talked about what I did with my time there. When I came back, I got one client with a million-dollar contract, and that client became my 20%. But now I actually knew what was going on. I still kept all my smaller clients because they were loyal to me and I was loyal to them, and it's not only about me. It's about adding massive value to the people that help me be where I am, and my clients are a very important part of that.

By now, I was looking at the world through a different filter. I didn't really believe in Pareto's law yet. I was just wondering if it was possible. So, when we acquired this big client, I had enough time to realize how the universe really worked within this context. I thought, *now that we have this revenue, let's try to reinvest it to grow in a better way.*

I started going on international trips. I thought maybe I could get clients in the US and South America since I already had employees in both places. It's funny, because I totally forgot about Pareto's law when it came to this. While I was busy travelling, I at least learned that I didn't have to be in my office all the time. I didn't have to be at the clients' office either. It gave me the freedom to start travelling knowing that my company was going to be okay. But I started making the same mistakes again in a different way.

I started going to all these trade shows and events all over the Americas, Europe, and even Asia to see if I could get clients! The same thing happened; the 80/20 rule. I acquired two clients, one in the states and one in Panama, and these two clients represented about 10% of everything I did. During this time, a lot of the revenue that we were making I was using to travel.

Quick sidebar: I fell in love with travelling. After Thailand, I realized that to travel is to live. My advice is to go as far as you can, as much as you can. Even going on airplanes, I know for some people is very troublesome. As I'm writing this, I just got out of a 20-hour flight from Toronto to Singapore with a layover in Taipei. But now we know how to do it, and it's lifechanging. I expanded my comfort zone so that travelling isn't really a big deal to me anymore. So that's the good side effect of the experiment that I did.

At this moment in my life, about July 2011 to December 2012, I spent a lot of my time travelling and hunting for opportunities. I was looking for ways to optimize my life using Pareto's law. But, like I said before, it was too much travelling, too much time and budget spent in trying to acquire clients in other parts of the world. I didn't consider that the US and Canada is where my focus should be. But you don't know what you don't know, right? By the end of 2012, we were finishing the project with a client that represented 80% of the company's income. Yes, I acquired more clients and it grew my revenue, but I was using most of the profits to travel to find more clients.

I realized that I wasn't completely fixed. Those first 30 days when I was recovering inspired change in my life. But it wasn't enough. As soon as I got this million-dollar client, I got a little cocky again. I got proud. When I started traveling, people looked at me in a different way, which fed my ego more, and **the ego is the enemy**. When you become proud, nothing works.

I didn't know this was happening to me. I just knew that I was selling contracts all by myself, and I was finally discovering myself as an independent entrepreneur. I had revenue coming in, and I had more developers. By this time, I had about 15-20 developers. But remember, a lot of those developers were for one client, which by the way, was the same mistake we made back in 2009-2011.

What I did was set myself up for another storm. The storm that was coming, in many ways, was bigger than the storms I weathered before when I almost had the heart attack. It wasn't so detrimental to my health, but it was worse because I had the tools I needed to prevent it, but I didn't really know how to utilize 80/20 properly, and my ego was still trying to take over. Now that I came out from a huge contract and a huge sale with a partner, I came back and was able to sell more than a million dollars by myself. **When ego sets in, you stop learning because you think you know everything.** On top of that, because I was applying the 80/20 rule, I thought I was the smartest guy in the room. The storm that was brewing because of that got me to another level of self-realization through pain.

The big lesson here is this**: knowledge is not power. Applied knowledge is power**. You have to execute. When you learn something, and you don't execute it, it's worse than if you hadn't learned it. It's worse to know what you need to do to be successful and willingly choose not to go down the right path. **Application is key**. Now that you've delved a bit into Pareto's law, you'll know what the most important actions are that you need to take in order to gain the maximum return with minimum effort.

Take a moment to think of something in your life that you've been kicking and punching to get. Is there a way to get 80% of what you want while giving 20% of the effort? If you do this, you'll find that you have more time in your life for fun stuff, like what I was doing.

I was travelling all over the world trying to get more clients, but the problem with that was that I wasn't enjoying myself. I was applying the rule, but I was always focused on sales and getting new clients. I was so hungry going to every conference and explaining to people what I did and how good we were that I was actually pushing people away. I wasn't enjoying myself. So, I was applying the rule for sure, but I was still broken inside and doing it for the wrong reasons.

I remember towards the end of 2012, my wife – by the way, I wouldn't be here if it wasn't for my wife. She is my foundation and she holds my existence together. She's one of the smartest people I know, and she's for sure way smarter than me! She analyzed me and just by seeing how I was she said: "David, stop it. When you go to another country, you don't even see it. All you do is talk about the conference and try to meet as many people as you can, and you try to sell as much as possible. Stop that, because you're not getting clients that way. If you decide to go to another conference, what you have to do is chill out. Try to add value to the people you meet, forget about what you do, and relax. Take time to visit the best places of the city that you're in. Relax, because you're wasting all this money and time trying to get clients and you're not getting clients anyway, and it's because you're too desperate for them. Try to see how you can help other people instead." When she said that to me, something in my heart started to change. That was towards the end of 2012. I started to realize there was still something wrong here, and that I needed to find what it was and fix it fast.

I still live my life applying the 80/20 rule, but the big difference now is that I know that there is always temptation to be proud and live with ego. It's like a cancer that you need to kill. There's a saying: *you have to kill the monster when it's a baby.* When it grows, it's a lot harder to kill it. This is what happened to me. I let a little monster grow because of my apparent success after flying solo. I let that small monster grow big, and it took me a lot longer to kill it.

## Golden Nuggets

- Ego is the enemy. **When ego sets in, you stop learning because you think you know everything.**
- Knowledge is not power. **Applied knowledge is power**. Application is key.

# 12

# Reality Check

*Staying humble, part two. How much is enough? How much do we really need?*

"Receive wealth or prosperity without arrogance; and be ready to let it go."

– Marcus Aurelius

It was December 2012. I had done at least 12 trips that year. I spent most of my net profits in travelling and trying to acquire more clients. I did manage to get two clients. One of them is still my client, so that was awesome, but it wasn't because of the travelling. That client came because of a referral! The other client was in Panama and we did well. It was just a single project. It doesn't compare to the amount of time and money I spent going to all these places, without seeing any real results.

Usually, Christmas time is a bit slow in the company because everyone is focused on vacations. I decided to take a couple of weeks off and just be home. I was trying to relax, but if you've picked up on the pattern throughout this book, I'm not a guy that can relax for a very long time. I need to be active and moving. You know, my wife says that I probably have a nuclear reactor in my butt because I can't stay still.

When I was at home, I was still checking on the company but watching lots of television. Christmas came and went, and it was the 26th when a famous TV show caught my eye. I had a few seasons to watch and I started watching it by myself.

My relationship with alcohol has had its ups and downs. If you remember what my doctor told me when I had the angina, I was drinking a lot and using the alcohol as a medicine without realizing it. Little did I know that I was doing something similar again. It wasn't as bad as it had been before, but I kept using alcohol. I never became an alcoholic, thank God, because I was born without that connection to addiction and I don't tend to get addicted very easily. But I was still abusing alcohol. I realized this because that evening, I remember bringing down a bottle of Jägermeister that we had left over from Christmas day. It was a brand-new bottle, and I watched this TV show the whole night. Before I knew it, it was 6am and the bottle was completely empty. I assessed myself, and I wasn't even tipsy. That really freaked me out.

By then, I had never lifted weights seriously or done any real exercise. I was 100% focused on the business. The next day when I woke up after having gone to bed at 7am, I felt scared. I realized I was still drinking too much alcohol. It was one of those moments where you feel enough pain to question what you're doing with your life. Still, after the first transformation, I was broken inside. The way I was applying my new learnings, like the 80/20 rule, was still ego-based.

I took a close look at myself after that and saw that I was completely overweight. I had a muffin top around my waist, my hair was almost gone and patchy with bald spots. I was almost 42 years old. I hadn't taken the time to slow down and take care of myself. I told my wife that I was going to stop. I looked for a program online.

At the same time, the big contract ended that month too, so I didn't have enough money to pay my staff in January. I didn't know what to do. The stress came back, and I was in bad shape again. I knew that what I had been doing up until that point wasn't working for me anymore.

I consulted my nephew, who was into health and wellness. He introduced me to this guy named Chris Gethin. If you want to do a physical transformation, I highly recommend this guy. You can find his stuff on the website bodybuilding.com. I saw that it was a 12-week transformation program. Chris Gethin is a body builder, but he let himself go because of an injury he had sustained. He was fat for about a year before deciding that he was going to transform himself. He recorded every single thing he did to change his body and turned it into a program that you can follow. It really resonated with me. I was fat and I had no idea how to lift weights, so I signed up for the program. I decided to go all-in on January 1st. I set a rule that I wouldn't be in my office unless I had gone to the gym first. I thought, *this is it. No more alcohol for me.* And I stopped, cold turkey. I didn't drink for the rest of the week. When New Year's Eve came around, we didn't throw a party and all I did was drink pineapple juice with my wife. It felt amazing because I knew it was exactly what I needed.

I got a gym membership and started on the video instructions from this program. It tells you what to eat, how to prepare your food, what not to eat (zero alcohol), and it required about an hour and a half at the gym almost every day. And there I was, doing it. The first day, I went to the supermarket and laid out all the healthy food I got and took a picture. I couldn't believe I was finally taking care of myself.

Something I realized was that the only way to achieve something is to find people that have already done what you want to do. I didn't have time to find a real person to mentor me through this, so I thought, *ok, I have the Internet. My personal trainer is Chris Gethin. I'm gonna try and find role models for business and life. While I'm working out on the treadmill, I'll start listening to these people who will contribute positively to different areas of my life.* I found spiritual leaders like Joel Osteen and Andy Stanley. I found business leaders like Richard Branson, and personal growth leaders like Tony Robbins. I was also listening a lot to Tim Ferriss. I had about five to six people that I could listen to every single day. As I started listening, especially to spiritual leaders, I started to realize that it was ego and pride that was bringing me down. Now I didn't have a partner, my company did great for a year and a half and now it was going down the drain again. I put in all this effort and nothing came of it. Even though I knew about the 80/20 rule, I didn't really understand how it worked within the context of a humble person.

As a result, I was supposed to do a 20-minute walk on the treadmill, and some days I ended up running for like an hour and a half or two hours and then I would do weight training. As

I was listening to these mentors online, I started to cry. One of the few things Tony Robbins has on YouTube are teachings on why we do what we do. I also heard a talk from Joel Osteen, and combined, I realized how focused on myself I was just because of the greed of getting material wealth. And I started crying. I understood the extent to which my spirit had been broken all this time. I knew these sessions roused something deep inside me, so I prepared by bringing a hoodie to hide my face at the gym in case I'd cry. When I cried, sometimes people would come and ask if I was okay. I was just fixing myself! I'd put up the hoodie and kept on running and listening and cry myself out. It made me feel new.

The transformation was 12 weeks, and the first three were spent crying. The more I was learning, the more I was crying. Sometimes I'd go from 6 in the morning till noon, because after the workout I'd go to the sauna and reflect on what I was learning, and then I'd get to the office. I took on this new routine and I stopped the travelling. I had three trips over the span of a few months, which was very little for the amount of travelling I had been doing regularly. I was just travelling for the people that were inviting me to go. I wasn't pursuing anything anymore. The contract that was about to end in 2012 got extended a little longer, so that gave me the time I needed to transform and keep the company afloat.

When I started, I was a little over 200 pounds. On the last day of the transformation, I was 159 pounds. I was measuring my body fat as well. I went from 29% to 10%. I couldn't believe it. The only bad side effect of this was that when my wife saw me at the end – she hadn't noticed exactly how much weight I lost because we saw each other every day – on the last day, I hugged her, and she said "Oh my god! You're too thin! I miss my teddy bear!"

The business was okay. It was paying the bills, but I was not generating any profit. I had completely lost my focus on profits. I was more focused on personal development. It started to change the way I was a leader too. I understood that I needed to become a true leader, not just a manager. **I learned that the behaviour of the people that work with you changes based on the leader's behaviour.** I started looking for leadership courses.

One of the conferences I went to in the United States was put together by something called The Society of Information Management, which I'm still a member of. They had a leadership forum that was like a post-graduate leadership program, but for technical people like me. It's basically for IT people that want to become VPs, CEOs or true leaders. I enrolled even though I didn't have the money to. I started going right after I finished my 12-week transformation. It was a remote course, but I had to be there every six weeks, and it was always in St Petersburg.

I got there, and I can confidently say it really helped me. They made me read 32 books. Every six weeks, we'd get together, and we had to present on each book. I was taught how to speak in public and how to deliver an impactful presentation. The leadership course was beautiful. I recommend it for anyone who has a technical background and wants to become a leader. They start with how to become the leader of yourself, and then they focus on how to lead a small team of 5-10 people, then a group of 100 people, until you're learning to lead thousands of people. It was life changing. It's called RLF, which stands for Regional Leadership Forum provided by The Society of Information Management, a multinational organization.

I focused on my leadership training and went back to the office. I was trying to maintain my current clients, keep them happy and work on all the responsibilities that come with running your own business, all while reading 32 books in one year. That was the catalyst for me, because before then, I never read business books. The only books that I read before were technical books, because I'm technical by nature. I'm a software engineer, so everything I consumed was to do with computer technology and nothing for leadership and personal development or business!

Once I read the books they assigned, the content and knowledge were so rich that it started to change my life. Now I read at least two books a month, and it's one of the best things that has ever happened to me. A single book could change your life with the knowledge and experiences of the people who wrote it. That's the only reason why I'm writing this book, because now I want to do my job and pass it on to the next generation. God has allowed me to have so many experiences in my life, positive and negative, that it's my duty and privilege to pass it on.

The graduation for the program was in Boston. It was in December 2013, and it was beautiful. The keynote speaker was Ray Croswell– he's the VP of Senior Development and Research at Google. He's a famous inventor and is the most accurate predictor of technology in the future. He actually predicted the

Internet, and he's also the inventor of the flatbed scanner. He gave us this amazing presentation.

By nature, I'm already a positive guy. However, Ray made such an impactful presentation on how this world is a better place despite what the news tells you. I decided to do more research on this, and that's how I found how Ray Croswell is friends with a guy called Peter Diamandis. He's the inventor of the X Prize, an organization that gives a prize to teams that are able to accomplish something significant. For example, Peter and the X Prize contributed greatly to the advancement of the space industry. They gave 10 million dollars to the first private company or group to bring a spaceship outside of the atmosphere and bring it right back.

Now, because I was used to reading, these are the first books I picked out myself:

1. Abundance by Peter Diamandis
2. Bold by Peter Diamandis and Steven Kotler
3. Exponential Organizations by Salim Ismail

I read these in 2014. I was already on my way to becoming transformed. These books gave me a completely positive outlook on life. Actually, Tim Ferriss recommends not to watch the news because the influence it has on an individual is very negative. It's a better idea to talk to friends, business acquaintances, and others and ask what's going on and get their perspective on it, rather than watch the news to understand what's going on in the world. Since then, I don't have the habit of watching the news, which is amazing. It's a cleanse.

In terms of physical transformation, once the twelve weeks were over, I continued going to the gym and doing weight training. It wasn't as intense as before, but I kept taking care of myself and watching what I ate. I don't have a lot of space to talk about this area of my life because it's taken me seven years to figure out the best way to stay in shape and how to pursue happiness through exercise and meditation. What I did with Chris Gethin was incredible for a massive transformation, but it's not sustainable for everyday life. I've accumulated tons of information over the years and it's helped me find what the secret to a happy healthy life is through wellness. This alone is the subject for another book.

My company wasn't growing, but I was growing as a person and my people started to realize that. What I realized, too, was that I had never focused on building a corporate culture. My spiritual transformation was huge, too, so I was so trusting in God that everything was going to be okay. I think 2013 was the only year where we lost money in the company. But it was the best year of the company because I took all this time to become a leader. I was still focused on myself and my self-development, and I noticed that the people in my company got happier. I didn't do anything different except focus on my personal growth and people came to work happier. Economically, however, shit hit the fan in December 2013.

By that time, the million-dollar client was gone, and I wasn't selling anything other than projects gained through referrals. We didn't have enough money for payroll that month. But I was relaxed. I wasn't stressed. I remember Marlene, my office manager, was worrying. She said "David, what are we going to do? It's Christmas and we don't have enough money. How are we going to pay all the people?" She told me this on December 15th. You know what I told her? I said, "I don't know, but I do know that we have a bigger God up there that controls the universe, and we're going to be just fine. We'll figure it out. Don't worry." We usually do payroll before Christmas, so people can have money for the season. When she talked to me, she was almost crying. The following Monday, I came back, and Marlene was still crying, but it was different this time.

She was crying happy tears. She hugged me, and I asked her what was going on. She told me, "David, we just got two big checks from the government. It's so much money that we can pay payroll for this month and next!" I was in shock! I thought it was a mistake, but there was no mistake. She showed me the checks.

The Canadian government has something called Research and Development grants, and we had filled out an application that to this day continues to help us grow our business. It was an internal tool to maximize time tracking, time estimation for projects, and I applied two years in a row, in 2010 and 2011 for the credit, but I never heard from them again. The last interview they gave me was in early 2012 and I had forgotten about it. It took them all that time to approve it, but when they did, they approved both years at the same time. I got all this tax money back and that saved the company!

The point I want to make is that I was not worried throughout all of this. If you know me, you know I'm a worrier, and I still am.

That's why I continue to work out and meditate because I know that's one of my biggest weaknesses. During the time this all went down, I had grown so much physically, mentally, spiritually and emotionally that I had an absolute certainty that everything was going to be okay. And by a miracle, everything *was* okay. We could pay everybody, and we had an amazing Christmas.

I still didn't have many clients, but I knew it was going to be alright. Funny enough, 2014 comes in and I realize my people are extremely happy. We don't have much in sales, but we still have smaller projects. The people were happy, and I wanted to know why. This is when I learned about something called culture. I started reading books on culture and spent all of 2014 learning how it works.

Another thing we did at the beginning of 2014, even without any money, was give back. We had never given back as a company before. So, with purpose, I looked for a charity in Canada that helps Guatemalan children in extreme poverty. Sure enough, I found Linda, the founder of Loving Arms. They were about to open a school in Guatemala. I asked her how I could help. She said, "Well, my vision is to provide breakfast to these kids. We're about to get approval to open this school, and we're going to have about forty kids coming. I know they won't come with any food. I know we can't teach them if they don't have any food in their bellies." I replied, "I don't know if I can pay you for food every single month because we're not too stable right now, but I'll do whatever it takes to provide meals for the kids."

I communicated to everyone in the company about the new initiative we were taking. We did this through an application called HubLinked that was made by us to build our company culture. As I was reading about culture, I was building this cloud-based program that allowed us to share everything in the company privately like our own personalized company Facebook app. People started to get excited.

I couldn't believe that in the times when we had the least money, we decided to give back. The minute we started giving back and shared it with the team, that's the minute the company culture started to grow exponentially. Suddenly, there was something greater than us, and we were working towards an important cause together. I didn't even realize this was happening. Now it's 2019, and the school grew from 40 kids to 100, and last year alone we provided breakfast and lunch to all the kids. We're now about to sponsor 19 kids personally and through the company, so not only do we provide meals, but we rallied together as a team to provide 19 children with an education. The more we do with that, the happier we get as a team. That was the foundation on which the culture changed. It's about adding massive value without expecting anything in return. That's a big part of being happy. **When you only focus on yourself and you grow, you get success, but you don't get fulfillment.**

When we got the government check, we had enough money for another month of payroll, and in that month, one of my old bosses back from 2004 called me up and said he had a big problem with his laboratories. He was the VP of science for a local company and he asked me to see if I could help out. Actually, we got the contract and they're still one of our biggest clients! So, 2014 was the year of growth.

If you want to focus on growing your culture, the book Leaders Eat Last by Simon Sinek is an amazing place to start. Then move to Tony Shay's Delivering Happiness. Then, read all of Richard Branson's books. When I focused on my culture, my company began to slowly grow. My focus was not growth anymore. I said to my wife, "Ok, I know that if we don't grow the business, it's going to eventually die because either you grow, or you die. The goal is 5% growth a year. That's it." I decided to live life fulfilled every day.

I began travelling again, but this time with the advice of my wife. I was adding value, trying to be happy, and not looking for that sale but looking for self-improvement. I wasn't spending as much money as I was before because I became more conscious of that. I kept working out, and I only focused on improving the culture and the HubLinked platform to knit the company even closer together.

Eventually, we got another client and were able to breathe a little easier. Funny enough, **when you focus on your people, your people will take care of your clients better.** That's one of the most profound breakthroughs I've ever had. Before, I was only trying to take care of my clients that I forgot to take care of my people. When your people are happy, your clients are going to be happy, and that is profound. I got that wisdom from Richard Branson.

We kept improving strategy and culture. Imagine what you can do with an amazing strategy and an outstanding culture. Those are now the two main focuses of my life. How can we improve the strategy to give more value to our clients' software development services, and how do I improve my culture so that the people are happier every day and fulfilling their own personal growth and destiny? That's what my passion is about now.

Now, in this chapter of my life, what I want is to expand that to the world, because if it worked for me, I believe it could work for everyone who wants to run their own business. It could work for whoever wants to bring people out of poverty and into the middle class and beyond. That's what entrepreneurs do. They create companies, and those companies employ people and create a better life standard for the people that are hired. That's what we need most in this world right now. We have enough multinationals. We have enough huge corporations. Those are fine, but a country gets richer when the middle class gets richer. Actually, according to The New York Times, Canada in 2019 just surpassed as the country with the richest middle class, and in the same year, we won best country to live in. That's what I wish for the rest of the world, not only Canada.

Remember how we just wanted to grow 5% per year? Instead of selling, I just became an advisor to people, so I would entertain any leads and try to add value by teaching them how to grow their business if it was in my field of expertise. It was always entirely up to them if they wanted to do business with me or not. As a result, my company started growing 15% per year, then 20%, until last year in 2018/19, we grew 100%. I couldn't believe it when I saw those numbers. I'm still applying the 80/20 rule, and I'm living life on my own terms. As I'm writing this book, I'm walking on the treadmill overlooking the skyline in Singapore. I couldn't be more blessed and fulfilled. I can, there's always a new level, but right now I feel happy, humble and in a beautiful state.

Every month brings new and different problems. We're just coming out of the best year of our business, and a few big projects are finishing up and we need to replenish those projects, but I'm in the process of that. Now I know that I have the certainty in my heart that the big guy up there is looking after us, and whatever His will is what's going to come. **When you realize that you're not in control, when all you can do is the best for other people, there's nothing but good stuff that will manifest in your life.**

I'm going to give you a story right now about how we started thinking about passive income. This topic is its own chapter in this book, and it's a very important one. As entrepreneurs, we don't have anybody that's going to pay us pension, and we can't rely on the government because we're self-employed. You have to think of your future, too. You also have to have a level of maturity in your economical life, so you don't have to worry for the rest of your life. You can even leave a legacy.

In 2011/12, I was still in that big office in an amazing building paying thousands of dollars a month on rent. When I knew this million-dollar project was finishing, I started to panic because I had expanded the office so big based on my ego. Half of it was empty because we didn't need all of it, but in my head, I had the corner office with the view of the city on the highest floor. Then my smart, beautiful wife told me, "David, how many people come see you at the office?" And I said "Nobody. Maybe one person a year. We're consultants, so we go to the client."

Then she said, “Then why are you paying so much rent? Let’s just get a house with the rent money and run the office out of a house.” I thought it was a good idea, but I didn’t have the cash at the time for the down payment. She said, “Don’t worry about that. God will provide.” I thought she was crazy. How could we buy the house without having the money for the down payment?

She started looking all over the market, and she found this beautiful bungalow about five blocks away from the big office where I currently was. It was still in the best part of the city. She remortgaged our house to get the down payment for that house, and my rent was reduced by 80%! Instead of paying rent, I was paying a mortgage, so I was adding value to my net worth instead of spending the money. We moved into this small house that was more than enough for the five people that came to work every day. The house was a duplex so there were people we rented out the bottom half to which would add to the mortgage. I don’t think I was even paying anything out of the company for the mortgage because the tenants covered the monthly costs. 2014 was so easy, as well as 2015. It made our life better.

In 2014, we started travelling with my wife and kids. I’ll tell you more about that in the chapter on passive income because it’s closely related. I’ll tell you how to travel, and how to achieve financial independence which, for me, was one of the most incredible things that I was able to accomplish in my life.

## Golden Nuggets

- When you focus on your people, your people will take care of your clients better.
- Let go of control enough to stay calm through times of hardship. Life always works out or presents a solution.
- Look for ways to make passive income.
- **When you realize that you're not in control, when all you can do is the best for other people, there's nothing but good stuff that will manifest in your life.**
- **The behaviour of the people that work with you changes based on the leader's behaviour.**

# 13

# Transformation & Life Mastery

*Staying humble, living with less. Full delegation and networking for life.*

"All great changes are preceded by chaos."

– Deepak Chopra

You're in the spot light. There's a shining light that warms your body, and you feel fulfilled, happy, and satisfied. This is what this chapter is about. I'm going to show you how all the troubles and obstacles I've had in my business and personal life all accumulated into graduating into a new lifestyle. I call it life hacking.

I got this name from the *New Rich* movement. What is life hacking really about? Basically, it's living life on your own terms. If you learn how to live on your own terms without getting bothered by what other people think of you, you're going to be free. Most people are enslaved by their ego, because they care too much about what other people think. This makes them follow certain rules of society that make them behave a certain way, and that's when the rat race comes into play. What's the rat race? Go to school, go to University, get a job, get a partner, have kids, save for retirement, then retire and die. That's what the general rules are, and there's nothing wrong with that, unless you want to live life on your own terms, which is what I've been discovering throughout this whole experience.

By the way, if you want to become an entrepreneur and risk it all in order to provide massive value to your clients and employees, it means that you are set apart from this rule. This norm no longer applies to you. The problem is that most entrepreneurs still have that mentality, and they never get out of it. So, they still may be working on their businesses as though they're still employees and looking to retirement as a way out. When you learn how to live on your own terms, you realize that you don't need retirement.

One of the biggest misconceptions out there that I've seen based on my beliefs is the work-life balance. When people tell me, you have to have a work-life balance, I laugh because work is part of life. So, what you have to have is life balance. This notion that you wake up, drive an hour to your job, work for eight hours, and commute back, and then you have your life, is ridiculous. Those hours given are still part of your life. If you want to live a fulfilled life, you have to be able to learn that you can work really hard, but you can party hard at the same time. In the American mass employment population, only 33% of people are engaged with their work. People aren't spending all the time at work actually working. Out of the eight hours, the most they work is three and a half hours. The other five hours are spent at the water cooler, talking to people, browsing the Internet for stuff they shouldn't be browsing, and being unproductive. That's the average! Isn't that crazy? You only have to work three hours a day if you don't want to get fired and go unnoticed. If you work a little more than that, you get promoted. Those are the facts. That is the first thing that you start learning with the 80/20 rule. 80% of your results comes from 20% of the time spent working on the job.

If you know this rule, why wouldn't you, as an entrepreneur, put in intense effort for two or three hours, go work out, and then come back and visit a client, add massive value, and then go to a networking event and have fun? Then you can come home and have dinner with your family, and after maybe you want to browse a new opportunity on the Internet, and that's okay! What I just described is a whole day mixed with work and pleasure, and that's my life. The problem is when you're focused 24 hours on the business, or when you're focused 24 hours on nothing. Then, that's how your life becomes unbalanced. I can live in high intensity intervals. That's how I train my mind and body, and that's how I live my life. Once I'm working, I go all in and I have full focus. Then I stop and do something else – for fun, for training, or for meditation – and I go all in with the same intensity. That's how I go through life; I take advantage of all my time and stay productive while enjoying whatever activity I'm doing. That's how I've been able to grow exponentially. The basis of all this is the 80/20 rule, so that's one thing you really need to learn and apply to your life.

Let's go back to my story. The company started to grow beautifully. I wanted 5% growth and we were doing 15-20%. By now, I was a master of the 80/20 rule. I knew exactly how much work I needed to put in and that gave me a lot of free time. Then, based on my experience when I did my first month away from the office in 2011 – I pulled both my kids out of school as they were both about to go into their final exams. We left early May and came back in the middle of June (in Canada, exams start late June), and both kids, one in grade 11 and the other in grade 8, did amazing! I thought they were going to lose the year and have to do it over. But, no! We brought all the material they'd need for the month, my wife asked the teachers and principal what they'd be missing while they were away, and they were fine. They came back, wrote their exams, and might've done better than the kids that didn't leave. So that was another breakthrough in my life, realizing that these kids could travel with us and not miss out on their education.

In Canada, we love the cold weather up until December 31st. Once the holiday season has passed, it stops being charming and starts getting really depressing. Canada has a six month-long winter on average, but the last three months are nasty. In 2014, I asked my wife what we could do to escape the winter. Based on what we know about life hacking, and breaking out of the common mold, how could we take the kids and go somewhere warm? How many countries could we go and visit? It would be what we call a "working vacation". We fill our days with school and work and then go out to tourist around once we're done. It's the perfect balance. You might hear some people say,

"Never mix work with pleasure", but I believe it's a great way to enjoy life while keeping your responsibilities taken care of. I'm always mixing work and pleasure. That's the strategy. If you take off for a couple of months and you just have fun, you'll have no business when you come back. If you travel but bring all your business ideas and strategies with you wherever you go, you can still prosper. All it takes is to do what others wouldn't even think of doing. For many people, they're stuck in the social mold that tells them that they either have to choose between work or vacations. Life hackers know that you don't have to choose – it's possible to do both. That's the essence of **life hacking**. To find a life hack in almost anything, ask yourself, "How can I get the maximum result with minimum effort"? Apply all the laws I've been teaching you in this book.

We decided to go to Argentina. We had people working for us there. Argentina is a beautiful country; I've been there many times before – probably more than fifty. My kids didn't know the country yet, so it was a good option. My wife had the great idea to visit countries around Argentina while we were staying there. We ended up taking off for two months in the winter and we did Brazil, Argentina, and Uruguay. We had a beautiful tour. My wife booked the apartments on Airbnb and always made sure the place came with a good Internet connection, so we could stay up to date on all our responsibilities. While I was there, I was also visiting my people, so we were still working, but not the regular work hours that people impose on you.

You know where the eight-hour workday comes from? It comes from the industrial revolution. Before the Industrial

Revolution, we didn't have eight hours to work a day. Farmers had to do their work depending on when the sun was up. The eight-hour workday came when we started automating production with machines, and the owners realized they could have three separate shifts and have the factories producing 24-hours non-stop. So, don't be bound by this archaic cultural norm. We're past the Industrial Revolution, we now have robots working those machines and we're in the Information Age. We can change this, as long as we are willing to. Now, if you come to work and you work three hours and during those three hours all your doing is fucking around on the Internet, then you're going to need the other seven hours. But, when you work, and you focus when you need to focus, and you gain maximum results, then you're going to be fine.

The trip was fantastic. We came back at the end of April, and the kids were doing outstanding in their schooling. Based on what I learned from my leadership course, I kept doing my networking. But now, if you recall from my previous chapter, the networking evolved into just having the opportunity to meet other people and to see if I can give them advice because I felt I had grown so much that I needed to share this. It was a win-win. I would also visit my current clients, too, but it felt more like a social visit. I also kept working on the company culture.

Overall 2014 was a fantastic year. 2015 came around and I wanted to do it again. We ended up going to South-East Asia, and then we did five countries in Europe. We spent another two months away, and we did the same thing. I kept working, the kids did school online and we were hacking life.

As I'm writing this chapter, I'm still in Singapore and the way I'm working on this is by using the four-hour overlap with the North American time zone. I wake up early, have a coffee and hit the gym. Usually when I want to put big ideas on paper, I like to be moving. The fact that I'm walking makes my ideas flow. After this, I'm going for a swim in the rooftop pool of this beautiful hotel, and then I'll go explore. When 8 pm comes around, since it's 8 am in North America, I'm going to work two or three hours to make sure business is taken care of. Those few hours are going to be intense with maximum results. All the meetings with my clients, my people, and future prospects are being booked between 8pm and midnight Singapore time. It's crazy, because people don't even know that I'm here. I don't even tell people when I leave, because by now I'm so efficient, I don't need to be in the country to be able to have an impact.

It's liberating. This is how the world becomes your playground. Now you're free to do whatever you want. I'm still producing revenue, and still blessing my clients and employees. I'm able to continue adding massive value no matter where in the world I may be. I don't have to be in my office anymore! Now I go to my office because I want to be there, not because I have to.

I remember I came back from vacations last week and it was a beautiful ten-day vacation to celebrate our thirtieth anniversary with my wife, Shelly. We had a great time in Cancun, Mexico. I'm a scuba diver, and I love the sun and the ocean. I came back, and I found that I actually missed my office. When I came back, I saw everyone working away and felt the love that's among us.

I felt so grateful. I realized that this is in fact what I'm supposed to do in life. For me, having that mixture of going and coming, the variety makes me so happy. Being able to share my life with beautiful people like John, Marlene, Natalie, Jonathan, Becca and Herber – It's wonderful. It is truly a blessing. More so, having the privilege to work and be friends with beautiful people in eight other countries fulfills me. This is what my ISU family is all about.

I guarantee you that if you take the right steps and figure out how to add massive value in the market with whatever products or services your company is based on, you can do the same thing, because I did it, and I have a software consulting firm. By definition, I was supposed to be with the client, but that was a limiting belief. We created systems where we could meet the client remotely, which turned out to be better and more efficient than in person. We can record the meetings and ask questions later if something isn't clear. At the same time, with HubLinked (the software product we created to improve the company culture), I added more functionality into the software and now we have something called the Portal Hubs. Those hubs inside the software help us collaborate with our clients and developers. Meeting recordings and relevant documents and links are posted in the assigned HubLinked portal. HubLinked keeps us honest, transparent, and more efficient throughout the company. Most importantly, it eliminated the necessity for us to go and see a client face to face. At the beginning of a project, we're always planning, and we'll go over to the client. I actually really love to see my clients at the beginning of a project, but then after it's running, we manage everything through HubLinked. The clients notice how efficient that is. It took me fourteen years to get there, but it's possible. One of my goals with this book is to save you those fourteen years to freedom and condense them into less than a decade. You should be able to accomplish this. If I knew what I know now, I could a have done this within five years.

One thing you cannot stop doing as an entrepreneur is networking. You have to keep on networking and meeting new people, with the right intentions. True connections are the ones you get more business through. The other part is delegation. The only reason why I've been able to travel so much and still work efficiently is because I finally learned how to delegate. You don't know how long it took me to get the swing of this. I was still writing software in 2009! And that's because I was too scared to delegate.

I was taught to hire people better and smarter than myself, so they can do the job better than I can so that I can focus on growing the business. That's what my first delegation exercise was, and it freaked me out. But after I took the leadership course, I really learned how to delegate, and I delegated all my responsibilities down to the point that all I do right now is advising. I give advice to my employees and to my clients. Everything else technical and with operations, I hire smart and amazing people to run it all. They're happy doing what they do best. I also invest in their professional and personal development.

That's what allows me to live life on my own terms. That's also part of life hacking. If you read the Four-Hour Work Week, you'll see how Tim Ferriss did it, too. He didn't even have employees by the end of it all. He completely automated his business. At some point I thought about doing that, but then I realized that I love the human relationships, too. I love having people all over the place. We have people working with us in eight different countries! From Canada all the way down to Argentina. We also have some people working for us in Spain. And I love it! It brings so much variety and different cultures into the company. That creates more value for our clients. I think if my business was fully automated and I didn't have to talk to anybody, I would feel like something was missing. I wouldn't be as happy as I am right now.

The next chapter is the final chapter in the book. I discuss how I achieve financial independence, which, believe it or not, was not planned by me. Everything that happened with financial independence was based on the advice I got from my dad, my grandfather, my older brother, and, most importantly by the Grace of God. And I married somebody who is smarter than me and can see life in a different way than I see it, my wife, Shelly.

Get ready to see how full financial freedom is achieved.

## Golden Nuggets

- Break out of the social mold. The 8-hour shift is old news**. Find your freedom**.
- **Delegate** tasks to people that are better than you.
- Focus on what matters, and the rest will fall into place. Focus on company culture and leadership.
- Do what no one else is willing to do. That is where you find the rewards.

# 14

# Passive Income

*The secret of success.*

"Money is a terrible master but an excellent servant."
– P.T. Barnum

I'm going to start this chapter with a quote from my grandfather with whom I shared a name, David. One day before he passed away, he told me "Son, there is always going to be more people in the world, but the amount of land is going to stay pretty much the same. If you want to have financial stability in your life, focus on paying off your house first, and then get some real estate. That is always going to be valuable."

My relationship to real estate has been a blessing. Let's move back to 1998. That year, we did a full review with a consultant to make sure we were collecting all the taxes we could collect. We ended up getting a beautiful check from the government of $8,000 from taxes we hadn't claimed properly! We decided to put that money into buying a house.

Back in 1998, the houses we were looking at were between 90k and 150k. You could get bigger more expensive houses, but that was the average for the time. My wife got so excited and we started looking for our first house. We eventually found it. When that happened, my job and my consulting gig was not paying enough to pay for the mortgage unless my wife kept on working, but she was pregnant with my third child. The day my wife went on maternity leave, my night-time gig grew enough to pay for the mortgage. Miracles are everywhere.

We moved to this amazing house. We started looking for houses at 60k and we ended up buying a house that was 140k. It had four bedrooms, a garage and everything else. That's why I couldn't afford it! In the end, I was able to make up the money at night and my wife stayed with the kids for a while before going back to school. We had a great life in that house. We stayed in that house for about ten years and we couldn't find anything better, even though we had more income. The house was so nice that to get something better, we'd have to double the price. It just didn't make any sense for us. Until finally in 2007, when my business started to get more stable, we kept looking for houses and we found one! Stay with me here.

We had two options. We could sell our current house and grab all that equity and move it to the new house, or we could remortgage our house based on its new value and use that money for the down payment and rent out the old house. That's when my grandpa gave me that advice. Then I asked my dad, and my brother. My brother had done exactly the same thing before. They all supported the idea. I ran the numbers. Before, I had bought the old house for $140,000, and by then it was worth $225,000. So, we got all the money to pay for the 20%

down payment of the new house. We paid around $350,000 for the new house and it was much better. And so, we moved.

That was the first real estate investing that we did. That was our first rental home. We found a nice couple to rent it to. My wife decided to take care of this business – that's what it became, anyway. She's talented at finding good people and making sure that home renovations were done well. She has this incredible ability to do this in a very economical way. At this point, it had absolutely nothing to do with my business. We took a little risk there and we made sure that the renters were paying the mortgage for the new house.

Because of the expenses and everything else, I was still paying about $200 a month out of my pocket to cover the expenses for the old house. This was before the real estate crash. Then, it came, and thank God it wasn't as bad in Canada as it was in the US. We didn't lose much value in the property and we were still able to pay the mortgage for the old house through the renters, plus the money we were putting in. That was 2007 – 2008.

We kept doing this for a while. The company started to grow. After my crisis in 2011, I realized I had made all this money and reduced it again. All the net revenue that I was getting, I was wasting trying to get more clients. I had too much temptation to keep doing that, so I decided to leave a healthy cash flow reserve in the company that would last us between three and six months of runway in case we run out of clients, and then every penny after that I'd invest into real estate.

The next house we got was out of love. I remember my eldest daughter was married at this point, and they were really young – around 20. They were fresh out of school and had very little money. When they were renting, they were getting kicked out at the time because real estate was going up and so was the rent, so they didn't have a stable place to live. They also had a child, my granddaughter. Out of love, my wife asked me what we should do. We thought, "Let's buy a house for them and rent it to them!" We did this one through the company.

I then got some advice from my lawyer and accountant. They told me, "What you need is to set up a holding company. Don't do it through your main business because you want to protect the assets". I set one up, and the holding company borrowed money from the corporation, and we had enough money to use for the down payment of that house. We gave it to my daughter. Don't get me wrong, they were paying full rent. The only thing I wanted to give them was the stability knowing that they could stay there forever if they wanted to. It was a little less than market price, but they were paying, nonetheless. They stayed there a while and during all this, the company kept growing and shrinking. I was taking money out and trying to pay off this new mortgage to the point where it was all paid off in 2013. I was now gaining revenue. We had the personal house and the business house, not counting the one we lived in.

In 2013, I got invited to participate in a new construction in Toronto. It was very cheap, I remember. I only had to put $10,000 down and was given four years to pay the other $90,000. It was all on paper. I asked my wife if she was interested in investing in this. It'd be nice to have an apartment in Toronto. The idea was to live there when we retire because I've always wanted to move to downtown Toronto and have the city lifestyle. By the time construction was going to be finished, our youngest, Natalie was going to be going to University and we'd be empty nesters, so it was actually a viable option for us.

They gave us the condo. When we signed, it was $350,000 on paper. When they gave us the condo four years later, the condo was already $450,000. Just like that. Right now, the value of that condo is close to a million dollars.

Now with the rental money, we kept repeating the cycle. When I say we, it's my wife and I. Remember the story about how we bought the house for the office? These are all my wife's ideas. If you look at the past up until now, I'd say that 90% of the family net worth is from the real estate business. It became a real business, to the point that if you put all the mortgages together, and you put all the expenses together, my wife and I could retire at any time. In fact, we could have retired in 2014. **What's going to set you financially free is having multiple sources of income.** For me, I had the income from my company, and from the rental properties, but I still had to pay all the mortgages. So, the residual value was not that much.

Something happened to me back in 2004. One of my night consulting clients – it was a start-up that did cloud accounting software for schools – they were running into trouble back then. They couldn't pay for my invoices anymore. They asked me if I was willing to work for equity. I still love the two Founders. We're still friends, and I told them "Of course I'll work for you". They let me know they could very well go out of business, so it was a big risk. I told them I'd do everything in my power to help them get out of this. As a result, they gave me 5% of the company when it was about to go bankrupt. We kept working for them, and they actually survived that initial trouble. They found an Angel Investor and they injected millions of dollars into the company and made it much better. I also grew my team with them when I had my full-time business. The company was eventually sold in 2011, but we didn't get a big payout right away. We had to wait five years – the buyer had five years to pay us out. In 2014, I finished collecting the shares and after doing the math, I received fourteen times more money based on that investment compared to if they had just paid my invoices. That alone enabled me to pay for my own house, which I still live in, and it enabled me to have enough revenue in my personal bank account to become financially independent. Now my house is paid for, I'm collecting rental income, and after you look at all the income plus the residual, I'm financially independent.

Now, there are three different levels. A lot of these learnings come from Tony Robbins. I'm a huge Tony Robbins fan. This year, I got into the Tony Robbins Platinum Partnership. When I was going through my transformation in 2014, a lot of the material I used was from him. I remember one of the lessons was in finances. Tony talks about the three pockets to give you financial independence. He says that you have to have your security pocket, your growth pocket and your dream pocket. Now, where do you get all this money? You have to live below your means.

That's one of the problems we have in North America; most people live above their means. They have credit card debt; debt that is not smart. If it's business debt or investment debt, that's OK. But if you're spending more than what you earn, that's when you become a slave until you die. **If you want to be financially free, you have to learn to live below your means.** If you really look at it, you really don't need that much to live in America. Being frugal and knowing where your money goes is what will allow you to eventually become financially free. So, Tony said to live below your means and whatever's left over, you have to invest. You invest into three pockets based on your risk. You put portions into your security pocket, some percentage in your growth pocket (which is high risk), and some in your dream pocket. What is your dream pocket? It's the stuff that you want to do. For us, it's the trips with our kids. For some, it may be buying a nicer car, or a better house, or a boat.

Because of all the problems that I had with ego and with arrogance, I really learned how to be humble. I also realized that I lost my need for material possessions. I started appreciating experiences and relationships more. When you stop wishing for material things, you're free. You realize that having a beer with a buddy will give you more happiness than buying the next fancy car, or the next watch – by the way, I love watches, so I put some money for that in the dream pocket. And it's okay to raise your standards. I was employing this strategy by accident in 2013, before I had heard of it officially. I was doing it out of common sense. But now that I hear the strategy, I was very specific with living below my means.

For me, my security pocket is my houses, the rental business. My growth pocket is allowing me to become an options trader in the stock market. That's something that has taken me two years to jump into, and so far, I'm so chicken that I only just started to do real investing. That's because I found a coach in the platinum partnership with Tony Robbins.

There are many people that you meet there, and I met this lady who's an options trader and she's helping me out, so I'm finally investing real money. That's the high growth pocket, but it's also high risk, meaning you can lose it all. In fact, before I was getting drawn into the stock market, my high-risk pocket was my business. In your life, there's not going to be anything riskier than running your own business. Especially when you grow exponentially – when that happens is when you have the most risk of going out of business, because you grow your expenses so much that if the business dries up, you could lose it all. For me, I thank God for every month that we're still in business. As I'm writing this book, we'll have been in business for 14 years already, which has been a tremendous blessing. Statistically, I could have been bankrupt three or four times already. It's a miracle that we're here. It's not because of smarts or anything I could have done. That's why I believe in God and I believe we're connected by the universe. You can call it whatever you like, the universe, God, whatever. But there is a higher intelligent power that's running the universe and we're all connected to that. We think we have control, but it's not true. **Once we give up control, that's when great things begin to happen, and you lose your anxiety.**

When I got the payment from the investment in that Start-up company, you don't know how much fulfillment I got. If you look at people with my annual revenues and my net-worth, you'd look at me and think I should be living in a huge house in the best neighbourhood, with 10,000sq ft. that we wouldn't use anyway. We could really live rich, but the house that we live in right now gives me so much peace of mind and pleasure. The house is gorgeous. My wife has done so many remodels. It's everything we need, and we spend more than 7 or 8 months outside of Canada anyway. Why would I come and get a huge house with a huge mortgage just to show it off? It's still my dream to have a bigger house, maybe, because we could have more guests over. Also, remember, I got most of my happiness from experiences, not material possessions.

A big part of why we're considering moving out of this house and into a bigger one is because in Canada, we have a taxation rule where any capital gain from your personal house is tax free. For example, your house is now worth a million dollars (which is around where my house is), I could sell that house and keep the million dollars and not give a penny to the government. People use that as a strategy in Canada to create wealth. Imagine, you then go to another house, it grows in value, and you repeat. I've got a lot of friends in Toronto that have 3 million-dollar houses, so I tell them, "You're a multimillionaire". But then they tell me, "Yes, but if I sell this house, where am I going to live? Any other house is going to be about the same price". The only way to actually live rich and free is if I sell this house and move out East, or to the North West Territories and that's too cold. That could be a life hack. We could move to a South American country or to Spain. With three million dollars in a different part of the world, you live free for the rest of your life. It depends on what your priorities are. But the options are limitless.

This is what I want you to understand. The secret to financial independence is to learn how to live below your means and realize that you don't need a lot of money to be completely fulfilled and happy and to add massive value. I was reading a quote from Keanu Reeves yesterday, and he was saying that most of the money he makes, he gives away because he knows that the more money you make, the more stress you're going to bring into your life. Every penny that you make is going to demand physical, mental, emotional, and spiritual energy from you. The more money you make, the more exhausted you're going to become. It's where his priorities are and what he chooses to experience in this life. At the end of the day, we're all going to die. We're only going to take our experiences with us. If the multimillionaire Keanu Reeves thinks like that, imagine what we can do.

The problem with people nowadays is, again, they try to live above their means and find themselves completely in debt. And what for? To show off to others? If you look at the way I dress, I have a couple of blue jeans, buttoned shirts, or plain V-neck shirts. Simple! And I love the way I dress. It makes me happy, and that's the idea. Don't get me wrong, if you like to wear fancy things or indulge in other ways like that, for sure! Go for it, and all power to you. I like cars, too. I have two nice fancy cars and its part of what I'm passionate about, and I set aside money in my dream pocket to do that. I didn't take it out of my security or growth pocket. **The secret is to define what you want in life,**

**how much it's going to cost you, and get your investments to pay for it, not your daily hard-earned income.** That's where we are right now.

When we got these two cars, one for my wife and the other for me, our investments were delivering so much money that we were paying that out of the investments. I'm not touching my income. If you make a lot of money, you can do whatever you want, and that's what's called absolute financial freedom – to do whatever you want, as long as you want. I don't think I'm there yet, but I don't think I need to be there. The way I am right now, what else could I possibly want and need? You know what I want? I want to share my knowledge with the world, I want to bring people out of poverty and create more entrepreneurs and make people financially independent, which is the first level.

Let's say you need $4,000 a month to live. That would cover rent, food, car, medical, gym, and everything else. You become financially independent when your investments alone will give you those $4,000, and not your work. And that number can change depending on the person, of course. For some it's $4,000, for others its maybe $40,000, or $400,000 a month. That's up to you! The problem is when people have too many expenses in things they don't even enjoy anyway. When you become frugal and realize that the most happiness you get can be from experiences and not material possessions, you could become financially independent as soon as possible. And I've seen it. There are people who manage to become financially independent with $3,000 a month, *and that's in North America.* Imagine if you move to a place like Puerto Vallarta, Mexico, where the standard of living is 50% of the cost in Toronto. Then, you could live with $1,500 a month. And by the way, that city is in front of a beautiful ocean with gorgeous mountains, and some of the best food in the world! The beautiful part about investing, too, is that the more you invest, the more you learn, and the more you grow your recurring revenue.

A long time ago, I stopped measuring my net worth in millions of dollars. I measure my net worth in my recurring revenue, because that's what I get to spend. The legacy I'm going to leave to my family and to the world is the wealth of the real estate I've accumulated. Everything else, I'll spend on recurring revenue until the day I die, living life on my own terms. So, remember that has to be your goal. When people measure their net worth in millions of dollars, it's okay, but that could be invested in the stock market in a long-term investment, where they don't get any dividends. Or it could be stuck in a building that isn't giving them enough recurring revenue. **Millions of dollars are meaningless unless it generates recurring revenue for you.** For me, I don't care about how much money my balance sheet says I have. What I care about is how much cold hard cash I have in my bank account after taxes. That's the money I can spend on experiences and dreams. One of my dreams right now is having a property in front of the ocean. I've been thinking about it with my wife and it's something we really want to do. We want to buy one in Mexico, overlooking the ocean with mountains behind us, and sunsets every day. That's in our dream pocket, and I know we're going to get there.

## Golden Nuggets

- What's going to set you financially free is having **multiple sources** of income.
- If you want to be financially free, you have to learn to **live below your means**.
- You invest into three pockets based on your risk. You put portions into your security pocket, some percentage in your growth pocket (which is high risk), and some in your dream pocket.
- Once we give up control, that's when great things begin to happen, and you lose your anxiety.
- The secret is to define what you want in life, how much it's going to cost you, and get your investments to pay for it, **not your daily hard-earned income**.
- Millions of dollars are meaningless unless it generates recurring revenue for you.

# 15

# Live Life on Your Own Terms

*Epilogue.*

"The pen that writes your life story must
be held in your own hand."
– Irene C. Kassorla

I want to take a moment to really give you the lowdown on what the New Rich movement is. I've mentioned it a couple times throughout the book, but I think it's important that I leave you with a better understanding of this concept.

In life, we are often programmed from a young age to follow the pattern of slaving, saving, and dying. This means that the logical order of life should be going to college, getting a high paying job that you work hard in, and eventually earning your right to retirement in old age. While this may work for some, to me, this makes no sense. Tim Ferriss offers an alternative to this called the New Rich.

In this day and age, we have access to the greatest resource known to mankind: the internet. This has revolutionized the way we communicate, connect, and shop. We can reach audiences that we otherwise never would have been able to reach before and in quantities unheard of for independent businesses. This opens up the possibility of making money online without all the work it would take to do in person. So, the New Rich involves working minimal hours for maximum profits by automating your business. If you master this, you can go in and out of mini retirements instead of waiting till old age to reap what you've sown. It's completely possible and it lets you live for the present moment. The wealth of the New Rich is measured by the freedom you have right now rather than the money you've made throughout your life.

Traditional retirement doesn't have to be your end goal. In fact, I'd argue that it shouldn't be. Why would you waste your youth working unsustainable hours only to be too old to truly enjoy the fruit of your efforts? Why not work as efficiently as possible so that you can do all the things you want to do while you still can? Being part of the New Rich is redefining the standards so that you can live the life of your dreams *right now.* And this is the whole point of Breaking Out of Corporate Jail. I made this book so that others out there can see a different way of finding freedom. The world is changing rapidly, and the cookie-cutter life plan is becoming less and less necessary to pursue. There is much, much more to this, and I recommend that you delve into Tim Ferriss's books to set yourself in the right direction. There are infinite possibilities when you start thinking outside of the box and living life on your own terms.

However, don't be discouraged if you're someone who's calling isn't business. You can absolutely become financially independent without the entrepreneurial ambition. To give you an example, I'll tell you about my CFO, John. For him, starting a business wasn't his calling. John graduated with a BA in Business Administration with a specialization in Finance. When he came to Canada, he ran into some trouble with finding a job in his area. At the time, factory jobs were available, so he went to work in one. It was really tough because it had nothing to do with the knowledge he had. Later on, he even had a job that required nightshift hours. He went through a time where he would go from difficult job to difficult job, trying to just pay all the basics. He was stuck financially and mentally, and he wasn't being fulfilled. It wasn't until he started getting jobs that were closer to what he went to school for. He landed a sales and marketing job that gave him the opportunity to travel. But, financially speaking, things changed when he managed to start working for various companies – as a consultant! It gave him the opportunity to diversify not only his knowledge, but also his time. He liked being able to work in different places. That ended up being a good step forward toward accomplishing his own goals and to start growing financially.

At a time when I still couldn't afford a full-time CFO, I remember encouraging John to come work with me while he was looking for a new client. At one point, John ended up having four clients! He was not only applying his knowledge, but he became independent. He went from one source of income, to four, which gave him a piece of mind knowing that if one went under, he still had three other rivers to drink from. When you break the standard that is taught to you in school, you're free to play by your own rules. For John, this meant abandoning the traditional one-job-till-you-die status quo which opened up a world of possibilities for him. That is where fulfillment starts. Breaking out of that is also a way to contribute to the world – by sharing your unique perspective. John says that three things lead to fulfillment through your work: having the freedom to manage your own time, being able to enjoy what you're doing, while at the same time accomplishing your financial goals.

John emphasizes the importance of knowing where you want to be financially and sticking to the plan. Without a clear vision of what you want and at least an idea of when you want it, getting there becomes a matter of day-by-day progress to the eventual accomplishment of that specific goal. For example, John set a goal to pay off his house as fast as possible. The normal period is around 20 to 30 years, and John managed to pay it off in 13. His specific goal was to make it to that 10% of mortgage payment every year in order to pay off his house faster. Not only did he pay it faster, but he saved about $150,000 that he would have had to pay in interest. The only way John was able to accomplish that goal – without having a business – was having a goal and living below his means. John and I have known each other for almost 30 years, and he taught me a lot about living below your means. It's very easy, especially in today's society, to crave all these things that we simply don't need.

Speaking of financial goals, John is about to move out to Mexico as a partial retirement. At 59, John wanted to start looking for places that offer a high standard of living for less money, as a way to make retirement more affordable and more enjoyable. He found the best of both worlds in Puerto Vallarta, Mexico, where the cost of living is cheap, but also offers modern amenities. This mentality is what makes the New Rich movement what it is. It isn't about amassing insane amounts of wealth; it's about living life on your own terms. You can choose who you want to work with, decide how much or how little you want to work, and go anywhere you want, while still being productive.

I hope that my life experiences and all the books I've read and recommended will come to be useful to you. I've read at least 20 books on how to become financially independent because I was obsessed with that, since that knowledge is what gives ultimate freedom. Please invest your time. This book is a guide to other books, where I got all my knowledge and all the mentors I've been blessed with throughout my life.

It is my true hope and pleasure that you grab all this knowledge and you apply it to your life little by little. Set some goals for yourself, learn to live below your means, and become financially independent. Most importantly, live your life with fulfillment. Remember when I was talking about company culture? After all these years of struggling, of successes and failures, I finally realized that there are three elements to achieving sustained happiness. You have to live with gratitude, you have to grow in your life all the time, and you have to contribute. You have to give back. Our company values and my personal values are living with gratitude, growth, and contribution.

Thank you for all your time spent with me. It would be my pleasure to have a coffee with you or have a conversation online. All my information can be found on the next page. If I can save you a couple of years of struggle and hardship by having a conversation with you, that's what I'm about. I know that the only thing in the world that cannot be paid back is time spent. You can always make money back, but you can never get a minute back from your life. I appreciate the time you spent on this book, and I really hope you got enough golden nuggets from me to change your life.

Blessings forever,

David Mansilla

davidmansilla.com

*Over the years, I realized that there are only three things that give you sustained happiness. "The path to sustained happiness: Gratitude, Growth, and Contribution". This is what I shared with my team members and our culture is now better than ever. www.isucorp.ca*

# Golden Nugget Index

Chapter 3.

- You have to **create demand** first before you invest in whatever it is you're trying to sell.
- Don't sell yourself short; find someone with more experience and talk over big decisions with them. They will be able to offer you clarity on how to **get the best outcome** from a situation.

Chapter 4

- **Transparency** and **honesty** will always help you win. The **truth** will set you free.
- It's possible to find **success without sacrificing** your family life.
- Always go the **extra mile** and you will succeed. Others are complacent with what they do. If you're thirsty for **adding massive value**, nothing can stop you.
- You have to come from a **humble** and **grateful** place, not from an aggressive and arrogant position. You can still be successful like that, but you will never be fulfilled.

**Chapter 5**

- **Mentors show you what is possible**. They expand your mind and help you dream bigger. Our scope of possibility starts off so small until you talk to someone who's done what you thought was the impossible.
- The minute you start realizing that you can count on other people's time and intellect, you begin to build a real business – not only self-employment.

**Chapter 6**

- Having **expectations** instead of **appreciation** is the fastest way to lead an unfulfilled life.
- Do whatever you can to end relationships on good terms. All we have in our jobs and businesses is the **connections we make**.
- Realizing you made a mistake is the first step towards your personal growth.
- Use your consequences to reflect on how to make better choices in the future.

**Chapter 7**

- **If you know what you want and are willing to do whatever it takes to get it, you will always get it.**
- If you're waiting for the right time to jump into the business, it will never be the right time. You could try to manage to catch a wave in the market, but it goes up and

down all the time. If you wait and wait, you will probably never do it. Courage is doing what you need to do despite the fear you have. It's okay to be afraid but be courageous and do it anyway.

- Don't borrow money if you don't need it. Don't use somebody else's money if you do not need it. However, if you need it, borrow it because borrowing money when you need it and when you have it is easier than trying to borrow it when you **really** need it. When you really need money, nobody will want to lend it to you. When you're okay financially, you can negotiate better with the bank and they'll give you a line of credit, or an economic lease you can use when you're in trouble.
- Knowledge isn't power. **Applied knowledge** is power.

**Chapter 8**

- **If you're not growing, you're dying.** It's impossible to stay in the same spot. Either you're growing or you're moving backwards and shrinking. If you have mentors and you don't pay attention to what they're telling you, it's useless to have them. You have to conquer your fears and realize that everything is going to be okay.
- If you want to be an exceptional business owner, you must learn how to delegate and inspire your team to be the best they can become.

**Chapter 9**

- Never have a single client be accountable for more than 30% of your net revenue. If you do, the client ends, and your company goes out of business. A healthy amount is 25-30% max. You can have a large client, but don't let it be more than 30% of your revenue. If you do, you have to do whatever it takes to get another client to level it out. You have to have the risk divided into three or four different clients.
- If you're resourceful enough, if you grow to have nerves of steel, and you're an honest person, **you will eventually make it.**
- **You need to already feel successful to attract more wealth into your life.**
- Reputation is **everything**.
- Your mentors will not only teach you how to live your life better without making the same mistakes they made, but they will also give you the connections you need in order to achieve **breakthroughs.**

**Chapter 10**

- A breakthrough happens for two reasons: when you have enough **pain** or when you have enough **pleasure**.
- Don't let greed destroy what's really important in your life. Be aware of your **attitude** and **outlook**.

- There are ways to use your time and energy more efficiently so that you can achieve all you want to achieve without burning out.
- Never neglect your **health**.
- Never neglect your **family**.
- Never neglect your **spirituality**.

**Chapter 11**

- Ego is the enemy. **When ego sets in, you stop learning because you think you know everything.**
- Knowledge is not power. **Applied knowledge is power**. Application is key.

**Chapter 12**

- When you focus on your people, your people will take care of your clients better.
- Let go of control enough to stay calm through times of hardship. Life always works out or presents a solution.
- Look for ways to make passive income.
- **When you realize that you're not in control, when all you can do is the best for other people, there's nothing but good stuff that will manifest in your life.**
- **The behaviour of the people that work with you changes based on the leader's behaviour.**

**Chapter 13**

- Break out of the social mold. The 8-hour shift is old news**. Find your freedom**.
- **Delegate** tasks to people that are better than you.
- Focus on what matters, and the rest will fall into place. Focus on company culture and leadership.
- Do what no one else is willing to do. That is where you find the rewards.

**Chapter 14**

- What's going to set you financially free is having **multiple sources** of income.
- If you want to be financially free, you have to learn to **live below your means**.
- You invest into three pockets based on your risk. You put portions into your security pocket, some percentage in your growth pocket (which is high risk), and some in your dream pocket.
- Once we give up control, that's when great things begin to happen, and you lose your anxiety.
- The secret is to define what you want in life, how much it's going to cost you, and get your investments to pay for it, **not your daily hard-earned income**.
- Millions of dollars are meaningless unless it generates recurring revenue for you.

Manufactured by Amazon.ca
Bolton, ON